A PICTORIAL HISTORY OF WINSTON CHURCHILL

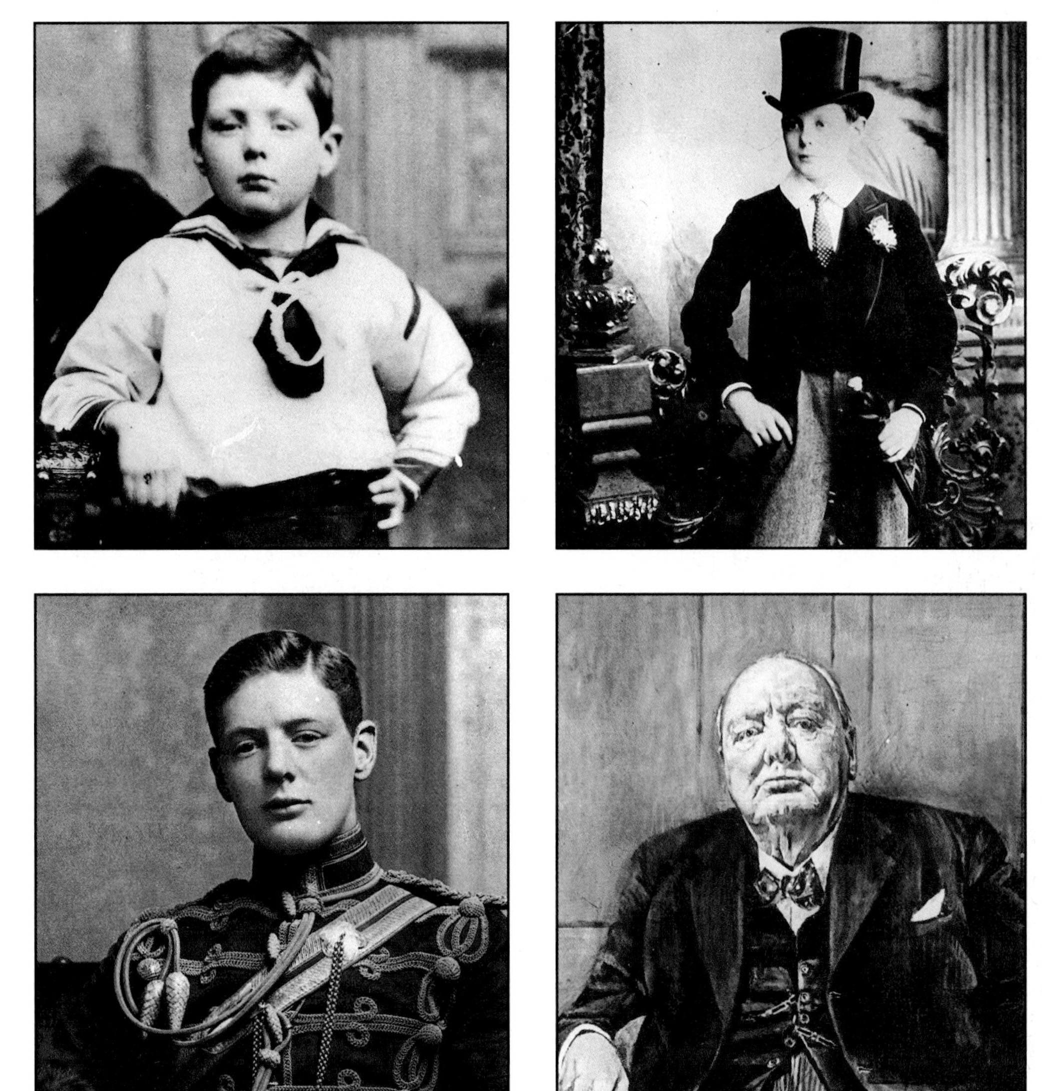

NIGEL BLUNDELL

PRC

This edition was produced in 1996 by the
Promotional Reprint Company Ltd
Deacon House, 65 Old Church Street
Chelsea, London SW3 5BS
for Chapters in Canada and Reed Editions in Australia

ISBN 1-85648-327-4

PICTURE ACKNOWLEDGMENTS
Every effort has been made to trace the ownership of all copyright material and to secure permission from copyright holders. In the event of any question arising as to the use of any material, we will be pleased to make the necessary corrections in future editions.

The following pictures were supplied by the Hulton Deutsch Picture Library: 7, 15, 17, 19(b), 28, 33(l), 35(r), 36(tr).
The following pictures were held by the Imperial War Museum: 6, 18, 21, 62, 64.

Printed and bound in Hong Kong

CONTENTS

Introduction

IF any single person can be said to have changed the course of 20th-century history, then that man is Winston Churchill.

He saved his country – and probably a continent – from subjugation.

He was a hero to the whole world, and one of its most recognisable faces.

Winston Churchill was a symbol of Great Britain in the proud days of Empire and the dark days of the Second World War. His bulldog visage became almost a caricature of the British personality at its most stubborn, unyielding, implacable but valiant best.

Yet Churchill's hour of greatness may never have come. A forgotten adventurer, a flawed politcian, he spent his 'Wilderness Years' outside the circle of power.

Happily for the free world, the summons to action came in time. The 'Bulldog' was unleashed. The tide of history was turned.

He promised nothing – nothing 'but blood, toil, tears and sweat'. But in Britain's darkest hour, he spoke of hope. His vision was uplifting.

'These are not dark days,' he said. 'These are great days, the greatest days our country has ever lived. And

LEFT: Churchill the war leader, like his German opponent Hitler, was also an enthusiastic painter.

ABOVE RIGHT: This statue erected in Churchill's honour in Deal, Kent, captures the defiant spirit that was vital to Britain's morale during the challenging days of 1940-41.

we must all thank God that we have been allowed, each of us according to our stations, to play a part in making these days memorable in the history of our race.'

The greatest part of all was played by Churchill himself. And when on VE Day, 8 May 1945, an elated Winston told the crowds, 'This is your victory;' they roared back, "No, it is yours!"

To paraphrase his own rhetoric, the world might rightly have said of Winston Leonard Spencer-Churchill: 'This was his finest hour.'

MAN OF DESTINY

WINSTON Churchill knew from the earliest days of childhood that he was born for greatness. His forebear, the duke of Marlborough, founder of his family's fortunes, had been one of the ablest generals in history – and 'history' was what young Winston respected most. It taught him the traditions and responsibilities of his proud family, one of the highest in the land. It taught him to accept unstintingly a boundless duty towards one's country. It taught him not to suffer fools, never to compromise. It also taught him lessons in tactics and diplomacy that stood his nation in good stead in its most desperate hours.

He was born in 1874 at Blenheim Palace, the magnificent Oxfordshire edifice designed by Sir John Vanbrugh for his ancestor John Churchill. He was given the palace, along with the title duke of Marlborough, by Queen Anne in appreciation of his great victory over the French and Bavarian armies at the battle of Blenheim in 1704.

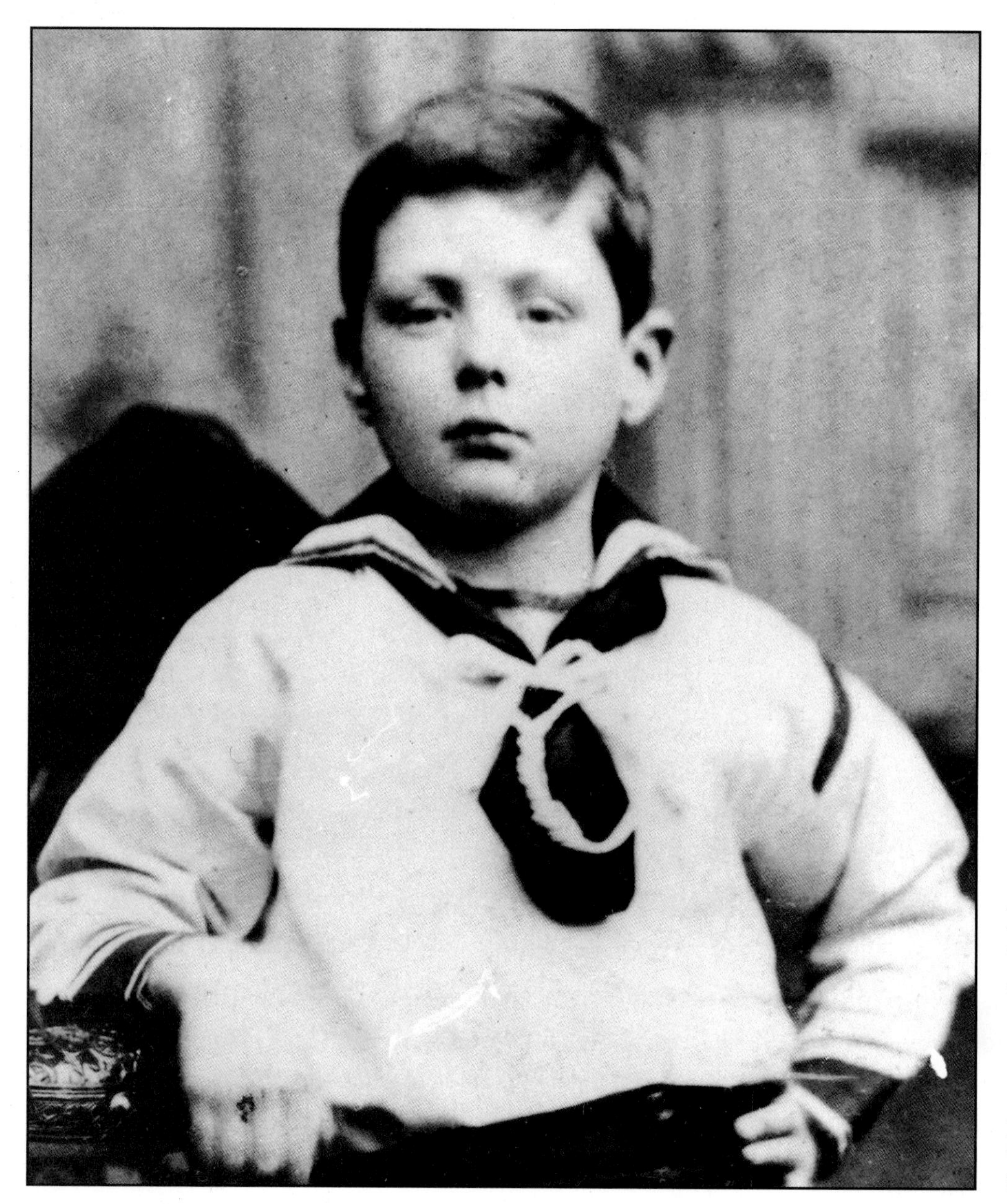

LEFT: The seven-year-old Winston Churchill was already being dressed for seafaring duties.

ABOVE RIGHT: He was sent to Harrow, one of England's elite public schools.

Winston was very conscious of his family's glories – 'glories of our blood and state', as he would later refer to them. It meant that, while many boys have only the vaguest ambitions, Winston had a rock-solid knowledge that he too must one day be ready to give all for his country. Soldiering was in his blood. Yet the great achievements of the first duke's career had not been matched by the succeeding generations.

Young Winston's view of his own destiny was tempered by the influences of his father and mother. His father, Lord Randolph Churchill, was a politician of huge influence in the 1880s. He was a compassionate but weak-willed man whose socially conscious policy of 'Tory democracy' appealed strongly to the newly enfranchised electorate of the later Victorian age. However, he was not a good party man; his determination to pursue policies at odds with the Conservative leadership's offered a lesson in how to lose political influence that his son did not always follow.

Mixed with Winston's English blood was that of his American mother, Jennie Jerome, undoubtedly the strongest influence in his young life. Jennie, daughter of the fabulously wealthy Leonard Jerome, brought much-needed hard cash into the Churchill family. She also brought a gentle and sensitive nature.

The birth of Winston, on 30 November 1874, was ironically typical of his entrances in later life: Winston arrived on the scene prematurely, noisily and with a great deal of inconvenience to all those around him. In fact, the baby was two months premature and the birth fraught with danger. Infant mortality was extremely high in those days and, being a Sunday, the child had to be delivered by a country doctor. The boy was very small but robustly healthy. He exercised his lungs to great effect.

Left: Churchill (left) with two fellow cadets at Sandhurst in 1894 – his lacklustre educational accomplishments forced him into a military career.

Above: This signature, with its prominent flourish, would become familiar to civil servants and world leaders.

His birthplace, Blenheim Palace, was not his parents' home; it was his grandfather's. Nor did his parents stand to inherit it. As younger son of the duke, Randolph had to settle for a comparatively much more modest home in London. There his parents entertained – Lord Randolph his political allies and Lady Jennie her social acquaintances. Indeed, they entertained in a style that the family could not afford. Lord Randolph was not poor by any standards of the day, but he was profligate all his life. Even though Jennie had brought an infusion of funds to the family, it failed to keep pace with Randolph's heavy spending and he never escaped the bonds of debt.

Baby Winston was largely ignored by his father– a pattern which was not an oddity in Victorian households, where fathers almost never visited the nursery. It was the relationship with his mother which was more peculiar. She undoubtedly loved her firstborn son yet treated him with seeming indifference.

Winston wrote of her: 'She shone for me like the Evening Star. I loved her dearly but at a distance.' And 'at a distance' is how she remained. Even by the standards of the Victorian upper class, she was a distant parent. As soon as a wet nurse could be found for little Winston, he was largely out of his mother's sight from one day to the next. The nurse, Mrs Elizabeth Everest, became the much-loved firmament in his young life. She continued to look after him through childhood, and it was Mrs Everest, not his parents, who provided the love and attention he craved.

So it was particularly traumatic for the small boy to leave his nurse and be dispatched to school. There were many times when Winston would cry himself to sleep and wish he was back home with Mrs Everest. But it was more than just homesickness. For St George's School in Ascot, Berkshire, ran a harsh regime; its headmaster, the Reverend Sneyd-Kinnersley, was reputedly a sadist.

Winston showed no academic promise at this early age and he found no favour with his teachers. His above-average reading ability irritated them, his weakness in all other subjects angered them. In years to come, Winston would remember how constant birchings failed to break his rebellious streak and how his school report concluded: 'He has no ambition.'

The grim two years at St George's affected Winston's health. It was the family doctor who stepped in and recommended the little boy attend another school. Winston found himself at a school in Brighton run by two spinsters. He stayed there until he was 13, never excelling at his schoolwork but a much happier child.

RIGHT: In 1910, at the age of 36, Churchill was one of the country's leading Liberal politicians. As president of the board of trade, he was involved in preparing the budget with the chancellor of the exchequer, Lloyd George.

It was the influence of the father he feared that enabled Winston to enter Harrow in 1888. The schoolboy had dismally failed his entrance exams – his Latin test paper was completely blank – and he was placed in the 'dunces' class. Attending the famous public school was not an opportunity Winston took advantage of. He was described as slovenly, unpunctual and careless. Beatings had no effect. Winston had become 'immune' to them after early schoolday experiences. In adult years he remembered his schooldays as 'the only barren and unhappy period in my life'.

Winston did shine in certain areas, though. His grasp of the English language was exceptional and he won a prize for his word-perfect recitation of 1200 lines from Macaulay's *The Lays of Ancient Rome*. He also became the Public Schools' Fencing Champion.

Neither of these accomplishments impressed his parents. They despaired of their son, whose only real talent – although one that ran in the family – seemed to be spending money. Jennie and Randolph held meetings to discuss Winston's future. He was not good enough to follow in his father's footsteps into Oxford

LEFT: Throughout his life, Churchill had a taste for taking a strenuous part in things. In 1911, he dared to risk his life in one of the newfangled flying machines.

RIGHT: In 1931 Churchill met the great American film star and director, Charlie Chaplin.

and thence into the world of law. The Church would not want him. It was Winston's love of playing with his toy soldiers that made his parents fall back on a third option: he would join the Army. So Winston was enrolled in Harrow's Army Class, which prepared young men for the entrance exam to the Royal Military Training College at Sandhurst.

This delighted the young Winston – but there was still one obstacle to overcome. Having neglected his studies, the Sandhurst entrance exams almost cost him his career. Special coaching from his Harrow headmaster were required before Winston scraped through at the third attempt. But so low were his marks that he failed to qualify for the infantry. He had to settle for what was considered the least intellectual branch of the forces, the cavalry. His father wrote him a vitriolic letter castigating him for not making it into a more elite force. It hardly mattered to Winston; he had just won the opportunity to step off what he called 'the path of purposeless monotony'.

LEFT: The moment of destiny – Churchill sits with his war cabinet in 1941.

LEFT: The Supreme Allied Commander, General Dwight D Eisenhower, exchanges views about the campaign in Normandy with the prime minister.

BELOW: The pinnacle of Churchill's career came on V-E Day when he, with his king, received the accolades of the crowd. Churchill had provided the vital spark to the war effort.

THE ODD COUPLE

Winston's family was not rich. His grandfather, the 7th duke of Marlborough, had not been in a position to provide a handsome allowance for Randolph, his younger son. This could have been the reason why Randolph proposed to beautiful American heiress Jeanette (Jennie) Jerome just three days after meeting her on a cruise ship.

Jennie's father, Leonard Jerome, was a self-made man, reaping his riches by brave gambles on Wall Street. He at first resisted his daughter marrying someone he viewed as a weak, foppish character. But Jennie's begging and Randolph's determination wore him down. The couple married in the chapel of the British Embassy in Paris in 1874.

It was not a happy marriage. Randolph had many affairs, yet Jennie stayed loyally by his side. No matter what trouble her husband found himself in, Jennie remained his greatest supporter. This loyalty was put to one of its greatest tests within three years of their marriage. Randolph threatened to expose the heir to the throne, the Prince of Wales, over a dalliance with a married woman. The scandal was hushed up but Randolph and Jennie were effectively deported to Dublin.

The young Winston was soon to hear rumours that his parents' marriage was somewhat unorthodox. Jennie had ended sexual relations

BELOW LEFT: Churchill's coat of arms from 1954 combined the Spencer and Churchill heraldry within the Order of the Garter.

BELOW: Lord Randolph Churchill, Winston's father, was regarded by Jennie Jerome's father as a weak, foppish character. His infidelities even in the early days of his marriage perhaps indicate Leonard Jerome was right.

with her husband when he contracted syphilis, allegedly from a maid. And in 1897, when Jennie gave birth to another son, it was no secret that the child was not Randolph's.

The Churchills' exile ended in 1880 and they returned to London.

Randolph, who had first entered the House of Commons in 1874, the year of his marriage, became a rising star in politics. He formed a breakaway Conservative group, the so-called Fourth Party, and gained a considerable following among the younger and more liberal of his fellow Members of Parliament. Rival politicians saw him as an adventurer, driven by his own ambition, but he silenced them by winning popularity throughout the country. When the Tories formed a government in 1885, Randolph was appointed secretary of state for India. The following year, at the remarkably young age of 37, he became chancellor of the Exchequer and Leader of the Commons.

Lord Randolph Churchill's fall from political grace was to be as fast as his meteoric rise. In 1886, he resigned over cuts in army spending. He did so in the arrogant expectation that he would be recalled to office to take up an even more elevated position. It never came. Instead, he returned with vigour to the 'career' of social butterfly, even renewing his friendship with the Prince of Wales.

LEFT: Jennie Jerome, heiress to a Wall Street fortune, was a prime catch for Lord Randolph Churchill. He proposed to her on the third day after they met.

ABOVE: IN 1908, Churchill became engaged to Clementine Hozier, the daughter of a distinguished war correspondent, Colonel Henry Hozier.

Randolph Churchill could still console himself with his empire-wide reputation as a statesman and a political innovator. When young Winston started Harrow in 1888, he was known as the boy with a 'famous father'. By the time Winston left Harrow in 1893, however, he had reason to be less proud of his father. Lord Randolph became prone to violent outbursts, more frequent and irrational as the syphilis destroyed his brain. Winston now felt confident enough to stand up to his father. Despite his vehement opposition, Winston joined the cavalry. And although father and son now mixed in the same circles, their relationship would never again be close.

The state of Randolph's health was now becoming obvious. His speeches in the House of Commons were incoherent and rambling, and at one point he had to be led from the floor of the Commons by a colleague to save him further embarrassment. He was diagnosed as suffering from 'general paralysis of the insane', a euphemism for the fatal sexual disease.

Jennie knew that her husband was dying. So when Randolph decided to embark on a world tour in 1894, she agreed to go with him out of a sense of duty, even though it meant being parted from her latest lover, Lord Wolverton. The trip was a disaster. At the end of the year, Randolph was brought home to his mother's house to die. He was 45.

Although huge debts had left Lord Randolph's son with a meagre inheritance, Winston felt really free for the first time in his life. His mother was now free too – openly to enjoy numerous love affairs. Jennie scandalised society by marrying a handsome guards officer, George Cornwallis-West, 20 years younger than herself. Their marriage broke down in 1913. Jennie's friends were even more shocked when, aged 64 she went on to marry an even younger man. He was Montagu Porch and in his early forties.

Jennie's death was particularly tragic. Determined to stay young at heart, the aging Jennie insisted on wearing fashionable high heels. It was while precariously walking down stairs in this unsuitable footwear that she fell and hurt her leg. Gangrene set in and the leg had to be amputated. She died of a haemorrhage on 29 June 1921. She had never been the the most loving of mothers, but she left behind a son who was almost inconsolable with grief.

When Winston heard of poor Jennie's death, he ran through the streets in his pyjamas to prostrate himself with grief at her bedside.

RIGHT: Churchill, here with his daughter Mary, built a house at his estate, Chartwell Manor.

BELOW: Churchill traveled to Colonsay in 1912 aboard the Admiralty yacht *Enchantress*.

IMPERIAL ADVENTURER

SANDHURST provided the young Winston with his first real feelings of self-worth and the opportunity to absorb information he could put to practical use. He was determined to achieve some degree of success and he worked hard and played hard, with the result that in 1894 he passed out eighth in a batch of 150. He developed a passion for horses and enhanced his leisure time playing polo and racing.

The young cadet was not to realise it of course, but during his Sandhurst days he made a political speech that was to be the first of many history-making orations. The Empire Theatre in London's Haymarket was

LEFT: Churchill's military career began as a subaltern in the 4th Queen's Own Hussars.

LEFT: During the Second Boer War (1899-1901) Churchill served as a lieutenant in the South African Light Horse.

LEFT: When the 4th Hussars were sent to India, Churchill resented being removed from the life he enjoyed among the social and political elite in England.

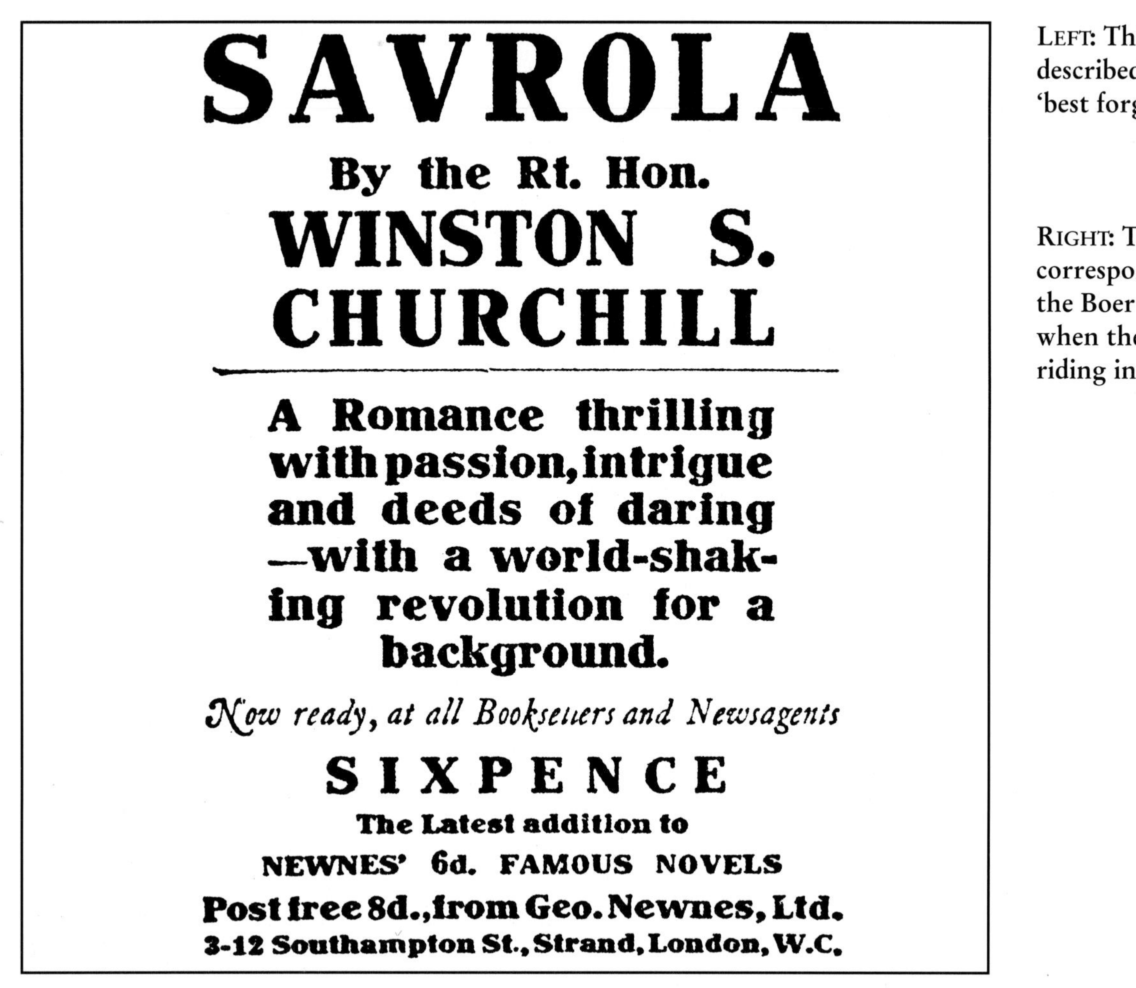
SAVROLA

By the Rt. Hon.

WINSTON S. CHURCHILL

A Romance thrilling with passion, intrigue and deeds of daring —with a world-shaking revolution for a background.

Now ready, at all Booksellers and Newsagents

SIXPENCE

The Latest addition to

NEWNES' 6d. FAMOUS NOVELS

Post free 8d., from Geo. Newnes, Ltd.

3-12 Southampton St., Strand, London, W.C.

Left: This first novel was described by the author himself as 'best forgotten'.

Right: The *Morning Post*'s war correspondent (far right) during the Boer War became a prisoner when the armoured train he was riding in was ambushed.

a popular haunt for Sandhurst cadets up in London. It also became the focus for a moral reformer, Mrs Ormiston Court. She objected to prostitutes plying their trade in the drinking area of the theatre and ordered that a screen be put up to ensure they kept their distance from decent people. Winston and his fellow cadets objected to what they saw as prudery. One night, drink having been taken, Winston and his friends tore the screen down and he delivered a speech about their actions. From that moment, Winston developed a taste for speaking publicly.

If Winston hoped to win some respect from his father after his successful time at Sandhurst, he was wrong. Lord Randolph had been incensed that his son had failed to qualify for the infantry. Now he was outraged at the cavalry's costs towards the upkeep of horses. It was an unnecessary drain on already stretched household expenses, Randolph stormed. Winston, once again, was on the receiving end of malicious scorn from his father. Lord Randolph called his son 'a mere social wastrel'.

In fact, Winston was never to have the chance of winning his father's affection. Lord Randolph died in January 1895. In March that year, aged 20, Winston joined the 4th Hussars as a second lieutenant. He revealed his ambitions to no-one, but Winston knew exactly where his future lay. He wanted to sit in the House of Commons, just like his father. He was wise enough to realise that reaching this goal would take time. He needed experience and he needed more money.

During the next three years, Winston saw garrison service in England and India but he was desperate to go into battle. For once in history, this was a relatively peaceful era and the only hope Winston had of seeing action was to join the war in Cuba. Here, Spanish regulars were fighting local guerrillas. Shamelessly using his father's name, and with just six months' service behind him, Winston arrived in Havana in November 1895. Finance came from acting as a war correspondent for the *Daily Graphic.* On his 21st birthday, Winston came under fire for the first time in his life. The fighting was slight and scrappy and Winston

£25.-.-

(vijf en twintig pond stg.)
belooning uitgeloofd voor
de Sub-Commissie van Wijk V
voor den Specialen Constabel
dezer wijk, die den ontvluchte
Krijgsgevangene
Churchill
levend of dood te dezen kantore
aflevert. —

Namens de Sub-Comm.
Wijk V
Lodk de Haas
Sec

Translation.

£25

(Twenty-five Pounds stg.) REWARD is offered by the Sub-Commicsion of the fifth division, on behalf of the Special Constable of the said division, to anyone who brings the escaped prisioner of war

CHURCHILL,

dead or alive to this office.

For the Sub-Commission of the fifth division.
(Signed) LODK. de HAAS, Sec.

NOTE.-The Original Reward for the arrest of Winston Churchill on his escape from Pretoria, posted on the Government House at Pretoria, brought to England by the Hon. Henry Masham, and is now the property of W. R. Burton.

Left: When Churchill escaped from a Boer prison camp, a £25 reward was posted for his recapture.

took no active part. But the experience satisfied his lust for danger. It also gave him his famous taste for Havana cigars.

Winston was by now setting the stage for his true ambition. He made sure he was seen at dinners and country house parties of the social and political elite. So it was with great reluctance that he followed orders to go to Bangalore in southern India. Most of his regiment treated the posting as a soft option. But Winston used his time wisely and to great satisfaction. When not winning polo trophies, he devoted his time to catching up on the education he felt he had missed. His nose was constantly buried in works of history, religion and philosophy. He devoured the words, his passion for learning newly kindled. Strong political and moral beliefs were stirring within him.

After an eight-month stint in India, Winston returned to England on leave. Not wishing to return to unstimulating Bangalore, his eyes alighted on reports of unrest among Pathan tribesman on the frontier between British India and Afghanistan. Winston engineered his presence there as a war correspondent and, despite his inactive status, deliberately put himself in the thick of the fighting. He took extraordinary risks.

On one occasion he was literally fighting single-handedly, firing a pistol at a tribesman just yards away. Relating the episode to his mother, Winston wrote: 'I play for high stakes and, given audience, there is no act too dangerous and too noble.'

Winston's brave though often needless brushes with danger earned him a mention in dispatches. Deaths of British officers left a 'vacancy' among the action, and Winston found himself willingly attached to the 31st Punjab Infantry Regiment, giving him his first chance of battle command. His overenthusiasm (or, depending on reports, his big-headedness) resulted in his being posted back to Bangalore after only six weeks.

HOW I ESCAPED.

MR. WINSTON CHURCHILL TELLS HIS STORY.

SIX DAYS OF ADVENTURE AND MISERY.

The ' Morning Post" have most courteously supplied us with the following story from their special war correspondent, Mr. Winston Churchill, relating how he escaped from Pretoria and found his way to Delagoa Bay, which he subsequently left by sea for Durban.

LORENCO MARQUEZ, Dec. 21 (10 p.m.).

On the afternoon of the 12th the Transvaal Government's Secretary for War informed me that there was little chance of my release. I therefore resolved to escape.

The same night I left the State Schools Prison at Pretoria by climbing the wall when the sentries' backs were turned momentarily.

I walked through the streets of the town without any disguise, meeting many burghers, but I was not challenged.

In the crowd I got through the piquets of the Town Guard and struck the Delagoa Bay Railroad.

I walked along it, evading the watchers at the bridges and culverts.

The out 11.10 goods train from Pretoria arrived, and before it had reached full speed I boarded with great difficulty, and hid myself under coal sacks.

I jumped from the train before dawn, and sheltered during the day in a small wood in company with a huge vulture, which displayed a lively interest in me.

I walked on at dusk.

There were no more trains that night.

The danger of meeting the guards of the railway line continued, but I was obliged to follow it, as I had no compass or map.

I had to make wide detours to avoid the bridges, stations, and huts, and in the dark I frequently fell into small watercourses.

My progress was very slow, and chocolate is not a satisfying food.

The outlook was gloomy, but I persevered with God's help for five days.

The food I had to have was very precarious.

I was lying up at daylight and walking on at night time, and meanwhile my escape had been discovered and my description telegraphed everywhere.

All the trains were searched.

Every one was on the watch for me.

LEFT: This account of Churchill's escape from the Boers was published in the *Morning Post.*

ABOVE: He returned to Africa in 1907 and wrote a book about his safari experiences.

LEFT: Churchill, at the time he began courting Clementine Hozier in 1908, was a man in the public eye – a Liberal member of parliament and the author of several popular books.

RIGHT: At the age of 64, Churchill still lived up to his adventurous youth. In April 1939 he was made an honorary air commodore and took a flight in a training aircraft.

Winston took the opportunity to write a book. *The Story of the Malakand Field Force* was completed in seven weeks, and Winston entered the literary world at the age of just 23. Flushed with success, he followed up with a novel, *Savrola.* It was, in his own words, 'best forgotten'.

Winston's reputation grew and in 1898 he was seconded as a subaltern to the staff of General Sir Herbert Kitchener's – despite that heroic gentleman's vehement refusal to accept a presumptuous young whipper-snapper into his service. The year was 1898 and Britain was seeking revenge for the death 13 years earlier of its colonial hero General George Gordon, speared to death by Dervish forces at Khartoum, in the Sudan. Kitchener was leading an Anglo-Egyptian army to retake the Sudan, and Winston had pulled a few strings to join the 21st Lancers in Cairo for the campaign. He had also managed to pick up various commissions as a war correspondent.

Winston arrived in Cairo on 2 August 1898 and exactly a month later was at Omdurman in the front line opposing the 50,000-strong Dervish army. Winston found himself in the middle of the lethal danger he loved – but it almost ended his adventurous career. The 21st Lancers, commanded by Colonel Rowland Martin, were ordered to kill fleeing stragglers after an initial battle which left thousands of Dervish fighters dying. Coming across a large group of Dervishes firing at the British from the crest of a slope, Colonel Rowland gave the order to charge – the last major cavalry charge in the history of the British Army. It was a terrible mistake. They rode straight into a hidden group of several thousand of their enemy. There was carnage as the lancers were hacked and slashed with swords. When Winston was set upon by three of the enemy, he shot himself out of trouble. He survived and, jubilant at fulfilling his romantic battle fantasies, penned a two-volume work, *The River War*, an in-depth examination of the Sudan campaign. He did not hold back criticism of what he saw as Kitchener's military failings.

Winston resigned his commission in 1899. He now earned enough from his writing to think seriously

Left: Churchill was an ardent imperialist throughout his political career, which brought him into conflict with the aims US President Roosevelt (second from left, with Free French Generals Giraud, far left, and De Gaulle), an equally ardent anti-colonialist, during diplomatic meetings such as this one at Casablanca during the Second World War.

Right: As Colonial Secretary, Churchill took an active role during the Irish treaty negotiations in 1922 that resulted in the creation of the Irish Free State and Northern Ireland.

about becoming an member of parliament. He was put up in a Conservative seat at Oldham but lost it by 1500 votes. Winston returned heavy with defeat to London. He was not to feel depressed for long. For news reached him that the war had started in South Africa.

Winston embarked on his adventures once more. He had managed to get the *Morning Post* newspaper to pay him the handsome sum of £250 a month to cover the war for them. Even Winston may have had reservations had he known what lay ahead.

There was a long history in South Africa of conflict between the Boer (settlers of Dutch origin) republics of the Orange Free State and the Transvaal, and the British in their neighbouring colonies, Natal and Cape Colony. In the end, the Boers stood in the way of British ambitions in Africa, and an increasingly tense diplomatic situation exploded into the Second Boer War on 8 October 1899.

One of Winston's first reporting assignments was as an observer aboard an armoured reconnaissance train near Ladysmith. The train fell into a Boer ambush and was derailed, only the locomotive remaining on the track. Winston, bullets and shrapnel whistling around his ears, helped load the wounded into the locomotive, which slowly moved off. The rest of the troops found cover behind the engine – until it gathered speed, exposing them to the enemy. The troops, including Winston, were forced to surrender.

Winston was held in a prisoner-of-war camp in Pretoria – but not for long. On the night of 12 December he escaped and, despite a £25 price on his head, made it to the safety of the neutral Portuguese colony of Mozambique. When he returned to Durban he was greeted as a hero and given a lieutenant's commission in the South African Light Horse.

Churchill saw much action in early 1900, including the bloody battle for Spion Kop, the relief of Ladysmith and the campaign in the Orange Free State. All the while, his reports were avidly read back home

Left: During the First World War, Churchill served in the trenches where he met Archibald Sinclair (left), a Liberal politician who would be his secretary of state for air in his war cabinet.

in the *Morning Post*. Some were highly controversial, justifiably praising the fighting powers of the Boers. Their marksmanship with modern rifles and skilful tactical sense time and again confounded the British generals better used to fighting native forces lacking modern military weapons. With the war all but over in July 1900, Churchill resigned his temporary commission and set sail from Capetown. He was done with fighting. It was time again to resume his political aspirations.

CLEMMIE

Winston was 33 when he met the woman who was to become his wife. Clementine Ogilvy Hozier was 10 years younger. Like Winston, she had suffered an unhappy upbringing. Perhaps it was this which attracted Winston to her. For, apart from one clumsy marriage proposal to an heiress, Muriel Wilson, who turned him down, Winston had little experience of women.

Clementine was unsure of who her father was. Her mother Blanche, eldest daughter of the earl of Airlie, had married Colonel Henry Hozier, a distinguished officer, war correspondent and later secretary of Lloyds. The marriage broke down and there was an acrimonious parting of the ways. Clementine could have been the product of any one of her mother's extramarital affairs. It was hard for Blanche to go through life as a social outsider. Clementine had no hope of her mother even bothering to introduce her to respectable society. But her beauty and good brain held her in good stead. She had been engaged twice before she met Winston.

Winston first saw Clemmie across a crowded ballroom while attending a function in London with his mother in 1906. He couldn't take his eyes

BELOW: Clementine proved to be the ideal politician's wife, able to withstand years of the relentless platitudes of platform speeches.

off her but was too shy to talk to her. It was not until March 1908 that they met again, at a dinner, and this time he summoned up the courage to approach her. Clementine was immediately smitten by him. She wrote that no-one could help but be 'dominated by his charm and brilliancy.'

The courtship was swift. Winston proposed on 11 August in the gardens of Blenheim Palace. Clementine accepted and they married on 12 September 1908 at St Margaret's, Westminster.

For Winston, with his fierce reputation, and Clementine, with her disadvantaged background, it was a strange but perfect match. They even had different politics, she being a true Liberal and suffragette sympathiser. But Winston, the great military hero, melted in Clementine's presence, calling her 'Kat' or 'Catkin' He was 'Pug' or 'Pig'.

The biggest cause of rows between the couple was Winston's way with money. He loved gambling and he loved spending. Even when he was made first lord of the Admiralty, money was tight. Clementine at first refused to move from their home in Eccleston Square, London, to the magnificent Admiralty House in Whitehall. She was worried about the cost of domestic staff. Their financial position grew so serious that in 1914, to pay household bills, Clementine sold a diamond and ruby necklace she had been given as a wedding present.

Their financial state was not aided by the birth of four children over a span of 10 years. Diana was the eldest, born in 1909, Randolph followed in 1911, Sarah in 1914 and Marigold in 1919. A fifth and final child, Mary, was to follow in 1922. But despite this bountiful family, Winston

BELOW: Clementine stands on the steps of No 10 with her husband and her only son, Randolph.

RIGHT: Clementine and Winston's grandchildren are gathered round on the occasion of his 77th birthday.

suffered deep depressions. It was with saddened frustration that Clementine found herself powerless to help her husband through them. The first of these 'black dog' states, which was to haunt him throughout his life, set in after the Gallipoli disaster. Clementine told friends she thought Winston would 'die of grief'.

Clementine too had been made ill on occasions, the cause being money worries, happily solved in 1921 when a family windfall provided Winston with an income of £4000 a year. But she had also had to cope with the war, four unruly children and a husband who preferred to spend holidays with his aristocratic friends. On these occasions he would set off to the south of France to paint, gamble and hunt wild boar. So Clementine was delighted when her husband asked her to accompany him on an official visit to Cairo and Jerusalem in March 1921.

The trip proved a great success. But it preceded a series of family tragedies. In April, Clementine's brother Bill committed suicide. Then Winston's mother died. They were still grieving when, in August , his youngest child Marigold developed a throat infection that turned into septicaemia. The little girl died.

Winston's windfall enabled him to look at grand properties. In summer 1921 he was shown around Chartwell Manor, near Westerham, Kent. The rambling house with its vast grounds fired Winston's romantic imagination. Clementine simply saw a dilapidated place that would cost a fortune to restore. Knowing there would be fierce arguments, Winston went behind his wife's back and bought Chartwell for £5000.

She may have appeared the downtrodden wife, but Clementine was very much a woman in her own right. She could be as stubborn or as

Above Left: Churchill, throughout his life, was dogged by periods of depression which Clementine could do little about. After his hopes for the Gallipoli campaign ended in disaster, she thought he would die of grief.

volatile as her husband. Once, during a heated argument over Winston's extravagant restoration of Chartwell, Clementine threw a dish of spinach, aimed right at his head. She also was infuriated by Winston's habit of seeking her advice on important issues then ignoring it.

Clementine often appeared in public for Winston. On one occasion, in October 1922, Churchill was struck down with appendicitis. It was a crucial time for him, for an election campaign had just got underway. Clementine, who had recently given birth to Mary, nevertheless travelled to Dundee to make speeches on Winston's behalf. Poor Clementine, dressed in her best pearls, was spat at by the town's women.

Clementine's devotion was boundless – she organised canteens for munitions workers in the First World War and Red Cross aid to the USSR in the Second. Her awards were a CBE in 1918 and a life peerage in 1965, when she took the title Baroness Spencer-Churchill of Chartwell – the name of the home she had so hated when she first saw it in 1921.

BELOW LEFT: The young Clemmie found Winston charming and brilliant.

BELOW: Clementine led as active a life as she could while raising four children.

POLITICAL WARRIOR

IN 1900 Winston Churchill at last successfully entered politics. He won the constituency of Oldham for the Conservative Party at his second attempt and spoke strongly in parliament on behalf of the defeated Boers. In 1904, his differences with the Conservative hierarchy grew, however, and he crossed the floor of the House of Commons and joined the Liberal Party. He was elected in their interest for Manchester North West in 1905 and gained high office as colonial undersecretary. His rise was meteoric. From 1908 to 1910 he held the prestigious post of president of the Board of Trade, after which he became Home Secretary.

It was while in this office that Churchill's love of melodrama plunged him into a minor adventure for which he was much criticised. A gang of Latvian anarchists, carrying out armed robberies in London, had killed three unarmed policemen. On 3 January 1911 some of the gang were cornered by police in a house in Sidney Street, Stepney. Churchill not only authorised the use of the Scots Guards and the Horse Artillery as back-up but insisted on being there to organise the 'Siege of Sidney Street' in person. When the house caught light, Churchill refused to let the fire brigade extinguish the flames, saying : 'I though it better to let the house burn down rather than spend good British lives in rescuing these ferocious rascals.'

Churchill became first lord of the Admiralty in 1911 as the storm clouds of the First World War loomed. He joined with the admiral of the fleet, Lord Fisher, in political manouevrings to fend off German ambitions to challenge British naval supremacy. Winston Churchill was the man of the hour. But his reputation evaporated with a single but major miscalculation.

Gallipoli, evocative of heroism and appalling loss of life, was to haunt Churchill for the rest of his days. It was the scene of an attempt to neutralise Turkey, Germany's ally, and link up with Russia by a great diversionary thrust at the enemy's back door.

Churchill believed it possible to attack the Dardanelles, forcing a passage to Constantinople (now

LEFT: Budget Day, 1929 – Churchill, as chancellor makes his way to the Commons with the historic red dispatch box.

OPPOSITE TOP LEFT: The new Conservative member for Oldham would, within four years, join the Liberals.

OPPOSITE TOP RIGHT: In 1904, at 30, Churchill could look on a parliamentary career that was beginning to blossom.

Istanbul), the capital of Turkey. In January 1915, the War Council authorised a naval operation to occupy the Gallipoli peninsula and sail on up to Constantinople. Churchill was not the originator of this plan but he made it his own. The Dardanelles became his obsession. He was convinced that if Constantinople fell, Russia would be reinforced, the Balkan countries would unite behind the Allied cause and that somehow this would lead to the collapse of Austria-Hungary and Germany.

But the campaign was a bloody disaster. Plans for the seaborne invasion were changed several times. There was poor organisation, delays and general misfortune.The coast was heavily fortified and after nearly a month of bombardment, the Anglo-French naval force ran into a line of uncleared mines. Three battleships were sunk and two others were crippled.

Any chance of success now lay with the army. But the landings on the Gallipoli peninsula were delayed until 25 April, by which time the enemy was fully prepared to resist them. The invasion force was pinned down on the beaches and there were heavy losses. The bold stroke was reduced to yet another episode of trench warfare, no different to the quagmire on the Western Front except for the weather. Churchill was blamed for the whole fiasco. He was no longer wanted at the Admiralty and in a new coalition government he was relegated to chancellorship of the duchy of Lancaster, a largely honorary title.

For the last 20 years Churchill had enjoyed a series of victories. Now he felt betrayed and humiliated. His pay was halved and his family were forced to move in with Churchill's younger brother Jack. He wrote: 'I feel like a diver too suddenly hoisted, my veins threatening to burst with the fall in pressure.'

Left: Home Secretary Churchill peers out from cover during the Sidney Street siege.

Churchill was not one to sit on the sidelines in wartime. After quitting Herbert Asquith's government, he followed brother Jack to the Western Front, joining the 6th Royal Scots Fusiliers. He made the move out of frustration; he certainly no longer had any taste for war or bloodshed. Indeed, as early as 1909 he had written to his wife after witnessing German army manoeuvres: 'Much as war attracts me and fascinates my mind with its tremendous situations, I can feel more deeply every year and can measure that feeling here in the midst of arms what vile and wicked barbarism it all is.'

Now his experiences in the trenches, where he saw several close friends cut down, compounded his loathing of conflict. When Churchill's battalion was amalgamated with another, he realised that he was far more useful back at Westminster. Happily, in 1916 Winston's long-time hero Lloyd George replaced Asquith as leader of the coalition government, and Churchill was made Minister of Munitions shortly afterwards. Put out of that job by the end of the war in 1918, he became secretary of state for war and air, then secretary of state for the colonies.

The 1920s were not good for Winston Churchill. After the fall of the coalition government in 1922, he tried and failed to win seats at Dundee and at Leicester West. With the Liberal Party in the doldrums and the Labour Party newly in power, Churchill, the Conservative-turned-Liberal next labelled himself an 'independent' to fight for the Abbey division of Westminster. Again he failed. Finally the Conservatives threw him a lifeline and he switched sides again, walking into their Epping constituency unopposed. He was given the thorny post of chancellor of the Exchequer from 1924 to 1929, during which time he engineered the rash return to the gold standard when the strength of the economy could not support it, and suffered the General Strike which followed hot on its heels.

Churchill treated the General Strike like a war. He spurned all attempts at conciliation with the trades unions. Instead he sent troops in to keep vital industries running and he launched a strike-breaking newspaper, the *British Gazette*, which reached a circulation of 3 million. The working class militants, whose strike he had helped defeat, never forgave him.

In 1929 he again found himself electioneering for the Conservatives, led by Stanley Baldwin, but by now the tide had turned against the 'old order'. Churchill retained his seat but Labour, under Ramsay

RIGHT: After the failure of the Gallipoli campaign, Churchill was forced from office. In order to play his part in Britain's war effort, the MP joined the 6th Royal Scots Fusiliers.

BELOW RIGHT: Churchill speaks to a public meeting on Britain's war effort. In 1916 he was plucked from the obscurity of the trenches to become minister of munitions in Lloyd George's coalition government.

MacDonald, became the largest single party in parliament and the ambitious Winston was ejected from office. It would be 10 long years before he came back in from the cold.

If the 1920s were tough on Churchill, the next decade almost destroyed him. Even when the 1931 election made the Conservatives the dominant party within the National government, Churchill was not invited to join. He was left to brood in the political wilderness, unable to influence world events, while Britain floundered under leaders he despised: Stanley Baldwin and Neville Chamberlain.

Churchill compounded his fall from grace with a controversial stand on the Abdication Crisis of 1936. He was deeply fond of Edward VIII and felt the king should stay on the throne. The establishment, church and general public did not necessarily agree. Later Churchill wrote: 'I was so smitten in public opinion that it was the almost universal view that my political life was at last ended.'

But Churchill was still on the backbenches throughout the 1930s, from where he was an eloquent prophet. Appeasement appalled him. Using his most powerful rhetoric, he cautioned the country about the

threat that Hitler posed. The *Führer* was giving tanks and planes to his armed forces in complete contravention of the controls imposed on the German military machine by the Versailles treaty that ended the First World War. 'I have watched this famous island descending incontinently, fecklessly the stairway which leads to a dark gulf,' he mourned.

Churchill was acutely aware of the scale of German military spending while others turned a blind eye. And he railed against the supine acquiescence of Chamberlain to the rearmament of Germany.

His forebodings were to no avail and he was rewarded with apathy and often ridicule. Only a small band of politicians backed him. The majority of British politicians and many of its people still clung to the belief that the First World War had been 'the war to end all wars'. Accordingly, national spending on ground, sea and air defence had been allowed to dwindle.

When Chamberlain bowed to Hitler in Munich in 1938, returning on 30 September with his notorious guarantee of 'peace in our time' – an agreement that allowed Germany to march into Czechoslovakia unhindered – the nation rejoiced. But Churchill described it as 'total and unmitigated defeat'. This declaration led to uproar in the House of Commons. When the hubbub died down, he continued:

OPPOSITE TOP LEFT: **He resigned from the Conservative shadow cabinet over his opposition to self-government for India's, yet still campaigned for the National coalition during the 1931 election.**

OPPOSITE BELOW LEFT: **His defection from the Conservatives in 1904 earned him the venom of Tory cartoonists.**

OPPOSITE BELOW CENTRE: **In 1915 *Punch* poked fun at the way he always seemed to be at the centre of home news.**

OPPOSITE BELOW RIGHT: **Churchill lost his seat in the 1922 election and remained out of parliament until 1924.**

OPPOSITE TOP RIGHT: **Churchill returned to the Commons in 1924, representing Woodford. He held the seat until the 1964 election.**

TOP RIGHT: **He painted this view of the Seine in 1930.**

RIGHT: **Churchill walks across the airfield at Croydon, on his way to France in 1939.**

> I do not grudge our loyal, brave people the spontaneous outburst of joy, but they should know the truth. They should know that we have sustained a defeat without war. And do not suppose that this is the end. This is only the beginning, the first sip, the first foretaste of the bitter cup which will be proffered to us year by year unless, by a supreme recovery of moral health and martial vigour, we arise again and take our stand for freedom as in the olden time.

While Neville Chamberlain was boasting of his achievment in containing Germany's threat to the European balance of power, Winston Churchill was preparing for the call he now knew was inevitable: his return from the wilderness and the beginning of his 'walk with destiny'.

LEFT: No 615 Squadron made Churchill their honorary air commodore in 1939, and he was flown in a trainer down to RAF Kenley to make an inspection.

LEFT: Churchill arrives for a state dinner at the Guildhall with the king and queen in June 1939.

That call came on 4 September 1939. Germany had invaded Poland three days earlier, in the knowledge that Chamberlain had, in July, guaranteed to defend the existing Polish borders. Chamberlain reluctantly declared war on Germany on 3 September, and offered the 65-year-old Churchill his former, cherished, wartime post as first lord of the Admiralty. The new war cabinet was announced on 4 September 1939 and soon the famous signal was being flashed to the fleet: 'Winston is back!'

FIGHTING TALK

Here are extracts from some of Winston Churchill's stirring war speeches:

I would say this to the House, as I said to those who have joined this government, 'I have nothing to offer but blood, toil, tears and sweat'.
13 May 1940

Victory at all costs, victory in spite of terror, victory however long and hard the road may be; for without victory there is no survival. We shall go on to the end, we shall fight in France, we shall fight on the seas and oceans, we shall fight with growing confidence and growing strength in the air, we shall defend our island, whatever the cost may be, we shall fight on the beaches, we shall fight on the landing grounds, we shall fight in the fields and in the streets, we shall fight in the hills; we shall never surrender.
4 June 1940

BELOW LEFT: The prime minister prepares to address the nation by wireless during the war.

BELOW: Spoiling for a fight – a Low cartoon shows the War Cabinet in a belligerent mood.

The Battle of Britain is about to begin... The whole fury and might of the enemy must very soon be turned on us. Hitler knows that he has to break us in this island or lose the war... Let us therefore brace ourselves to our duties, and so bear ourselves, that, if the British Empire and its Commonwealth, last for a thousand years, man will say 'This was their finest hour.'
18 June 1940

Never in the field of human conflict was so much owed by so many to so few.
20 August 1940

Above Left: 'All is going very well' – A Nazi poster distributed in occupied Belgium during 1940 suggests that Churchill's rhetoric was optimistic.

Above: The defiant spirit of the summer of 1940, when Britain stood alone against the Germans, is captured by this cartoon.

Far Left: The British Bulldog holds the line – a propaganda poster links the prime minister with a popular breed of dog.

Left: A 1942 forces postcard leaves no room to doubt Churchill's ability to inspire the servicewoman.

Daily Mail

FOR KING AND EMPIRE

NO. 13,743 — SATURDAY, MAY 11, 1940 — ONE PENNY

LATE WAR NEWS SPECIAL

ALLIES ADVANCING ON FRONT OF 200 MILES

B.E.F. Pour Across Belgian Frontier

VANGUARDS CLASH IN LUXEMBURG

BRITISH and French troops were last night advancing on a 200-miles front from the North Sea to the Moselle River. Britain's Mechanised Army guns, tanks, armoured cars, and men had reached points deep in Belgian territory.

The greatest air battle in history was still being fought over Belgium and Holland, and official announcements gave German losses

GERMANS' CLAIM:

'Allied Bombs Killed 24 Civilians'

'We Will Reply'

CHURCHILL IS PREMIER

All-Party Cabinet

By WILSON BROADBENT, Daily Mail Political Correspondent

MR. WINSTON CHURCHILL is Britain's new war Prime Minister. He took office last night after Mr. Chamberlain had handed his resignation to the King; until early this morning he was engaged in forming his War Cabinet of Conservative, Labour, and Liberal members.

He set about the task, with his customary vigour, immediately after exchanging places with Mr. Cham-

LEFT: An early report of the Allied counteroffensive in the West in 1940 gives no hint that the German thrust through the Ardennes would bring defeat, and the Nazis to the Channel's shore.

Daily Express

No. 12,579 — Monday, September 16, 1940 — One Penny

SETS THE SEAL ON ANY MEAL H·P SAUCE

R.A.F. smash Goering's Sunday raids on London by 400 planes

175 SHOT DOWN

Another bomb on Palace

5 RAIDERS CRASH ON LONDON

Fifth hospital bombed

SECOND WEEK OF THE BATTLE OF LONDON WAS OPENED BY GOERING WITH FOUR MORE BIG DAY AND NIGHT RAIDS—AND BY THE R.A.F. WITH A SMASHING VICTORY.

This morning it was learned that 175 enemy aircraft, out of 400 sent in many waves, were shot down in the three Sunday daylight raids on London. Thirty R.A.F. fighters were lost, but the pilots of ten are safe.

Again the Nazi murder bombers were sent against Buckingham Palace in a third deliberate attempt to kill the King and Queen. One bomb, which did not explode, damaged the Queen's private apartment.

Vengeance was swift. Almost immediately afterwards the plane which bombed the Palace was shot to pieces in mid-air by Spitfires.

Great air battles were fought out fiercely all the way from the coast to London as big formations of British fighters sailed into the massed squadrons which tried to fight their way to the capital.

Spitfires ambush raiders

SPITFIRES and Hurricanes, lying hidden in clouds, and working in perfect conjunction with ground batteries, darted from their sky ambush yester-

I WATCH THE

A story that must earn a man the V.C.

St. Paul's saved: 1-ton bomb

A MONSTER bomb weighing fully a ton which for three days has been buried near St. Paul's Cathedral in London, exploded yesterday—but not at St. Paul's.

The courage and tenacity of a bomb disposal section under Lieutenant R. Davies saved St. Paul's from being levelled to the ground.

STOP PRESS

BERLIN RAID ALARM —GERMAN VERSION

LEFT: The Finest Hour – Sunday, 15 September 1940, was the last day of massive German attacks during the Battle of Britain. As this headline indicates, the Germans suffered heavy losses, and called off their air offensive.

Give us the tools and we will finish the job [Addressing Roosevelt].
9 February 1941

Do not let us speak of darker days; let us rather speak of sterner days. These are not dark days; these are great days – the greatest days our country has ever lived. And we must all thank God that we have been allowed, each of us according to our stations, to play a part in marking these days memorable in the history of our race.
29 October 1941

This is not the end. It is not even the beginning of the end. But it is, perhaps, the end of the beginning! (After Allied victory in North Africa)
23 October 1942

Issued by the Ministry of Information  *in co-operation with the War Office*
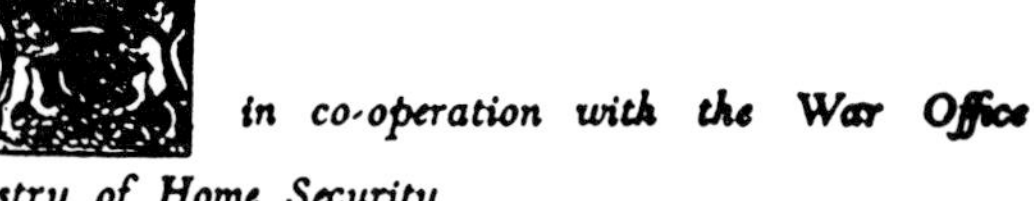
and the Ministry of Home Security

Beating the INVADER

A MESSAGE FROM THE PRIME MINISTER

IF invasion comes, everyone—young or old, men and women—will be eager to play their part worthily. By far the greater part of the country will not be immediately involved. Even along our coasts, the greater part will remain unaffected. But where the enemy lands, or tries to land, there will be most violent fighting. Not only will there be the battles when the enemy tries to come ashore, but afterwards there will fall upon his lodgments very heavy British counter-attacks, and all the time the lodgments will be under the heaviest

troops are landed in their neighbourhood. Above all, they must not cumber the roads. Like their fellow-countrymen on the coasts, they must "STAND FIRM". The Home Guard, supported by strong mobile columns wherever the enemy's numbers require it, will immediately come to grips with the invaders, and there is little doubt will soon destroy them.

Throughout the rest of the country where there is no fighting going on and no close cannon fire or rifle fire can be heard, everyone will govern his

LEFT: Churchill's message to Britons in that stern summer of 1940 encouraged everyone to 'play their part worthily'.

OPPOSITE: On a visit to an armaments factory, Churchill tries out a Sten gun.

BELOW: Manchester nurses receive an official visit from the prime minister in thanks for their work during the Blitz.

His Finest Hour

CHURCHILL took no satisfaction in being proved right about German ambitions. However, he set about the job of war robustly. His hatred of Nazism was well known, as were his loyalty and patriotism. He summed up his position with the words: 'I've only one aim in life – that is to defeat Hitler. That makes things very simple for me.'

The fire for the task which he possessed was sadly lacking in many of his comrades. The British military leadership fell into line with their French colleagues, who chose to wait for the Germans to attack. The ensuing months of relative military inactivity became known as the 'Phoney War'.

The first British action of the war was confined to the sea, so Churchill was where he wanted to be – in the thick of it. German U-boats and magnetic mines were causing havoc to the Royal Navy and merchant ships. A U-boat slipped into Scapa Flow, the anchorage of the British Fleet, just 10 miles off the Scottish mainland, and sank the battleship *Royal Oak*. Eight hundred of the crew died

Britain's first vital victory of the war was the sinking of the German cruiser, the *Graf Spee*, on 17 December 1939. The *Graf Spee*, which had been the scourge of British shipping in the South Atlantic, was

LEFT: Churchill and General Sir Edmund Ironside, the chief of the Imperial General Staff, leave the Admiralty building in May 1940.

LEFT: Churchill on his way to see King George VI in May 1940, during discussions over the formation of his war cabinet.

LEFT: The French prime minister Paul Reynaud (right) met with Labour leader Clement Attlee, General Sir John Dill and Churchill in Paris in June 1940.

BELOW: Churchill pauses to exchange old war stories with an air raid warden who fought against the Boers.

engaged by three Allied cruisers: Britain's *Exeter* and *Ajax* and the New Zealand vessel *Achilles*, and after a day of action, the battered German hulk limped into Montevideo.

Uruguay being neutral, Montevideo's port facilities were available to Captain Hans Langsdorff for three days only and German appeals for an extension were rejected. Wrongly believing that more Royal Navy big guns were on the way, Hitler gave the order to scuttle the once-proud ship rather than see her fall into enemy hands. Captain Langsdorff could not live with the shame; three days later he draped himself in the flag of the Fatherland and shot himself.

Although the victory was pyrrhic, Churchill seized the opportunity to trumpet it with a victory parade through the streets of London. Another incident illuminated an otherwise disastrous start to the war. In February 1940 HMS *Cossack* raided the German supply ship *Altmark* in the waters of neutral Norway and released 300 prisoners taken by the *Graf Spee* months before. The raid was highly illegal, given Norwegian neutrality, but won the full approval of adventurer Churchill.

In revenge, Hitler ordered the invasion of Norway – and it was the British reply to that invasion that cost Chamberlain his post as prime minister.

On 2 April 1940 Chamberlain announced that Hitler had 'missed the bus' in Europe. Britain's position was secure, he assured parliament, in the wake of a string of trade agreements with the Netherlands, Belgium and the Scandinavian countries. A week later Hitler began a full-scale invasion of Denmark and Norway. The turn of the Netherlands and Belgium would come shortly.

The Royal Navy was in the midst of mining strategic Norwegian waters and the arrival of the Germans took them completely by surprise. British and French troops embarked on a defence of Norway some weeks later but it was by and large a shambles, for which Churchill was mainly responsible. Yet Chamberlain carried the can. Leo Amery, a long-time political ally of Churchill, rose in the Commons to repeat the words

LEFT: Enthusiastic crowds cheer the prime minister during a wartime visit to Merseyside.

TOP RIGHT: Churchill's top brass during the war included Air Marshal Portal (seated, far left), Marshal Alanbrooke (seated, left) and Admiral Cunningham (seated, right).

RIGHT: The war cabinet poses in the garden of 10 Downing Street.

Left: Churchill gives his famous V-for-victory sign during a visit to Sheffield in November 1941.

Right: Brendan Bracken, Churchill's behind-the-scenes fixer and spin doctor, consults his notes during a visit to Bradford.

Below Right: Churchill inspects the ruins of Coventry cathedral, destroyed by German bombers in November 1940.

of Cromwell on the dissolution of the Long Parliament in 1649: 'You have sat too long here for any good you are doing. Depart, I say, and let us have done with you. In the name of God, go!'

A vote of confidence in Chamberlain, although successful, was not sufficiently overwhelming to allow him to stay. Tory rebels wanted a coalition government but Labour refused to join under Chamberlain's nominated successor, Lord Halifax. Churchill's hour had come.

Before parliament, new Prime Minister Winston Churchill outlined his government's policy: 'It is to wage war, by sea, land and air, with all our might and with all the strength that God can give us; to wage war against a monstrous tyranny, never surpassed in the dark, lamentable catalogue of human crime.'

Churchill was also leader of the House of Commons and minister of defence. The chiefs of staff reported to him. Into his Cabinet came important men from outside parliament – newspaper baron Lord Beaverbrook and trade union leader Ernest Bevin. There was at last a sense of cohesion and purpose about the government inspired by Churchill's dictatorial leadership.

If Churchill was the saviour of his country, it was in the first few weeks of his premiership. For Churchill refused to entertain the idea of a negotiated peace, no matter how bleak the prospects seemed. During the last weeks of May 1940 there was a suggestion of a treaty between the enemies, with Mussolini acting as go-between. Many leading British politicians were seduced by it, including Halifax. Even Chamberlain was tempted. But Churchill, supported by Labour's Attlee and Greenwood, was implacably opposed.

Churchill was soon confronted with one of Britain's biggest disasters of the war. The losses of men and equipment on the beaches of Dunkirk in May and June 1940 might have been enough to destabilise a weak leader or to revive talk of peace. Yet it was hailed as a victory. The British Expeditionary Force, numbering

about 200,000, was sent to France during the onset of hostilities. After months of inactivity, it was quickly hounded out of Europe by German forces when they stormed into the Netherlands, Belgium and France. There was a dramatic race for the coast. The vast majority of the British Army and the best of its equipment was about to be swallowed up by the enemy.

The commander of the BEF, General Lord Gort, knew there was no option but to withdraw his men by sea, a plan that was clearly fraught with danger. Privately, many, including Churchill, believed only 20,000 would escape the clutches of the Germans. Hundreds of men fought a courageous rearguard action to stem the tide of the *Wehrmacht*, knowing they were doomed. Ironically, the men on the beach at Dunkirk also received a valuable helping hand from Hitler who delayed the advance of his tanks in order that the slower German infantry might catch up.

Operation Dynamo, the evacuation from Dunkirk, began on 26 May with Royal Navy and French ships braving the inadequate port facilities to pluck thousands of troops from danger. The public was told about the crisis on 31 May and thousands of small craft took to the seas to join in. A staggering 338,000 British, French and Belgian soldiers were brought out alive. Behind them lay devastation. BEF soldiers were forced to abandon 63,900 vehicles, 289 tanks and 2472 guns, leaving the British Army critically short of weaponry. There were decaying bodies littering the sand and shallows. Thousands were left behind. Those who returned were furious at the lack of training they had received and blamed the Royal Air Force for much of the tragedy of Dunkirk. Churchill once again escaped the recriminations.

Criticism of the RAF was unwarranted. Its fliers were in action over Dunkirk, often far away from the desperate gaze of those stranded on the beaches. During the hopeless Battle of France, the RAF lost nearly half its strength in fighter combats and bombing raids. And as the summer of 1940 waned, it was to face the toughest challenge yet from Hitler.

RIGHT: On the rifle range – Churchill examines the marksmanship of some soldiers.

LEFT: The prime minister visited a bomb-damaged neighbourhood of Bristol in March 1941.

RIGHT: During an inspection of a Commando base in Scotland, Churchill witnessed a demonstration of wireless equipment in action.

LEFT: Churchill attended the 'Big Three' conference with Stalin (left) and Roosevelt (centre) at Tehran in 1943.

RIGHT: The prime minister was greeted by other members of the war cabinet at London's Paddington station on his return in January 1944 from conferences in Cairo and Tehran.

First the convoys sailing through the Channel were the targets of the German air force. Then Fighter Command's air fields came under attack. The third phase was a blow at the civilian population of Britain. London and other major cities were bombed day after day, then night after night.

Churchill refused to move to the safety of the countryside, although he no longer slept at 10 Downing Street. Indeed, he courted a certain amount of danger by insisting on watching from a rooftop as torrents of bombs fell from the skies. His aides were told: 'When my time is due it will come.' On one such occasion, an air raid warden approached him.

'If you will kindly excuse me sir, would you mind moving?' ventured the warden.

'Why?' Churchill muttered.

'Well, sir, the building is full of smoke and you are sitting on the smoke vent.'

Churchill was touched by the relentless courage of the RAF pilots. Likewise, the plight of those living under fire in London and other cities left him choked with emotion. As often as possible, he visited the bombed areas. When he inspected a shattered air raid shelter in which 40 people had been killed the previous night, a huge crowd awaited him and he was mobbed as he left his car.

'Good old Winnie!' came the cry. 'We knew you would come. We can take it. Give it 'em back!' Churchill broke down, unable to hide his sobs.

LEFT: In September 1942 Churchill saw the new tank which had been given his name.

RIGHT: Churchill and General Montgomery confer on a damp day in 1944.

There was a less charitable side to his nature, however. Air Chief Marshal Sir Hugh Dowding, in charge of Fighter Command, was the brains behind the Battle of Britain. It was his economical use of planes and pilots which saved the day. Dowding was a cautious man who considered all the options before committing himself. Churchill tended towards throwing everything he had at a situation to resolve it.

Dowding and Churchill had fallen out during the Battle of France when Dowding refused to allow the prime minister to send still more fighter squadrons to the Continent. Despite Dowding's later success, Churchill could not forget this act of wilful disobedience, rational consideration of which might have led to the conclusion that he was wrong and Dowding right. When the Battle of Britain was won, instead of receiving grateful thanks, Dowding was sacked.

Churchill, having successfully punished Dowding to gratify his own ego, then developed a taste for sacking his military and naval subordinates, particularly those whom he thought were faltering in the field. As the war progressed, the list of victims grew: Peirse (from Bomber Command in 1941), Wavell twice, in North Africa (1941) and Southeast Asia (1942), Auchinleck in North Africa (1942) and Tovey (from command of the Home Fleet in 1943) and Harwood (from the Mediterranean Fleet in 1943).

Italy declared war on Britain in June 1940, opening new fronts in the Mediterranean and Africa. All seemed gloom to the generals but the first glimmer of real victory revealed itself to Churchill. British and Commonwealth forces in Africa crushed the Italian army, and might have conquered Libya had Rommel not turned up in Tripoli in January 1941.

LEFT: Churchill, watched by a solicitous Montgomery, climbs into a DUKW amphibious lorry during his visit to the Normandy beachhead in June 1944.

RIGHT: Churchill makes the journey across the Channel in a destroyer in June 1944

BELOW RIGHT: Montgomery escorts the prime minister to his jeep at the start of the tour around the Normandy beachhead.

BELOW FAR RIGHT: Churchill is shown around a destroyer at sea in early 1941.

Churchill could not resist getting involved in Greece following an invasion of that country by Italy. Obsessed as he was by history, he revelled in the prospect of preventing the 'cradle of Western civilisation' from falling under Italian control. Yet this intervention – Churchill's idea although he was to punish Wavell for it – ended in another disaster as Hitler fished his Axis partner Mussolini out of the mire.

The Greek episode was a disastrous one for Britain and the Allies. Once Hitler had sent his armies into Greece, their victory was swift. The defenders were driven to the island of Crete, which was also then overrun by a daring German airborne assault.

There were distractions elsewhere in the war which prevented close inspection of Churchill's strategy. On 10 May 1941 Rudolf Hess made his mysterious flight to Britain. Hitler's deputy was apparently hoping to negotiate peace with the king through Britain's duke of Hamilton. Churchill was as perplexed by the bizarre event as anyone. He held back from cashing in on it as propaganda for fear it was a Nazi ploy.

Later that same month came the sinking of the *Bismarck*, seen by Britons as a sweet revenge for the loss of HMS *Hood*, the pride of the British fleet. *Hood* had been sunk by the German ship on 24 May with the loss of almost all of her 1300-strong crew.

June brought the entry of the Soviet Union into the war on the Allied side. Hitler broke a peace pact forged between himself and Soviet leader Joseph Stalin in spectacular fashion when he invaded with a massive force of men and machinery. Churchill was one of many who had warned of the impending attack. Stalin had refused to believe him.

Churchill was fervently anti-Communist but he now prepared to support Stalin's battered armies any way he could. He announced: 'No-one has been a more consistent opponent of communism than I have for the last 25 years. I will unsay no word that I have spoken about it. But all this fades away before the spectacle which is now unfolding. Any man or state who fights on against Nazidom will have our aid. Any man or state who marches with Hitler is our foe.'

Britain was still fighting for its survival. Churchill knew that the entry of the United States into the war could only result in victory. US President Franklin D. Roosevelt was sympathetic to Britain, but many

LEFT: Under the watchful eye of the prime minister, commandos rush ashore during an exercise.

BELOW: Churchill chats with General Sir Alan Brooke, the chief of the imperial general staff, about the progress of Operation Overlord.

RIGHT: Churchill flashes his *V*-for-victory salute as he departs on another energetic inspection tour.

BELOW: Two nurses, collecting for St John Ambulance, get a donation from a VIP.

LEFT: **Churchill returns the greetings of American servicemen aboard the *Queen Mary* on his arrival in the US in 1943.**

Americans still clung to their longstanding tradition of avoiding involvement in Europe's 'squabbles', and believed that no European war was worth an American life. Roosevelt himself was a devout anti-colonialist, and his enthusiasm for the British cause would lessen if he thought the only result of US intervention was to prop up British imperialism.

The two leaders met in August 1941 and signed the Atlantic Charter, an agreement in principle that aggressor nations should be disarmed. Soon American involvement became full-blooded.

On 7 December 1941 the Japanese launched a surprise attack on Pearl Harbor, killing more than 2400 US servicemen and destroying 18 ships. Churchill was nothing less than delighted. He wrote: 'To have the United States at our side was to me the greatest joy. Our history would not come to an end... I went to bed and slept the sleep of the saved and thankful.'

In the wake of US entry into the war, Churchill made a visit to the White House. His British bulldog appearance and extrovert character were happy eye-openers to the American public – and to the president himself. One day Roosevelt steered his wheelchair into Churchill's room to find the British Prime Minister dressed in nothing more than a towel. Roosevelt instantly apologised and made to leave. Churchill recovered his composure and insisted he stay, saying: 'The Prime Minister of Great Britain has nothing to conceal from the President of the United States.'

Crucially, even before the Japanese attack on Pearl Harbor, Churchill had managed to get American military planners to agree to deal with the threat from Germany as a priority before turning their entire might on Japan. The visit to Washington confirmed this as well as deflecting one of his major wartime failings: the hopeless exposure of the British Empire's eastern flank.

LEFT: A company of US soldiers receive a high-level inspection in the spring of 1944.

BELOW: Churchill stands outside Montgomery's headquarters in Normandy with Sir Alan Brooke (left) and Monty (right).

Left: Top brass cross the Rhine in March 1945. Churchill walks on German soil.

Right: The prime minister is briefed during a visit to the 8th Army fighting in Italy.

Churchill had insisted that the battleship *Prince of Wales* and battle cruiser *Repulse* were sent to Southeast Asia in late November as the crisis in Japanese-American relations worsened. They were not provided with adequate air support; and on a sortie to attack the Japanese landings in Malaya, both ships were sunk by bombers. Far from being 'an impregnable bastion', as Churchill imagined, Singapore and the other eastern colonies were inadequately defended by men who were poorly trained and painfully ill-equipped. This allowed the Japanese to march into Hong Kong, Burma and Singapore with extraordinary ease.

Later Churchill protested he did not know that the defences of Singapore had been so perilously weak. He had undoubtedly been told but he postured instead of taking action. 'The little yellow men will never dare to challenge the might of the British Empire,' he once foolishly bragged. When proven disastrously wrong, Churchill, without necessarily blaming himself, descended into a bleak depression.

If Churchill made some poor judgments during the war, he also made some which were sound and saved countless lives. As 1942 opened, the Americans were pressing for a second front in Europe. Stalin was likewise eager to see the Germans come under some additional pressure. Churchill held out against the idea. He knew that any invasion mounted without sufficient planning, supplies and men would be a disaster. Instead, he favoured a landing in western North Africa. That plan was adopted and the Torch landings, which took place soon after Britain's glorious victory at El Alamein in Egypt, opened a second front in North Africa that resulted in forcing the Germans out of Africa once and for all. As Churchill said jubilantly: 'Before Alamein we never had a victory. After Alamein we never had a defeat.'

Nevertheless, Stalin remained deeply unhappy. The Germans had some three million men fighting on the Eastern Front, and barely a hundred thousand in North Africa. A landing in northern France would alleviate the German pressure on the Red Army. The tension which had long existed between Churchill and Stalin was never more strained than when the British prime minister visited Moscow for the first time in August 1942, as the Germans advanced on Stalingrad.

'When are you going to start fighting?' Stalin goaded. 'Are you going to let us do all the work? You will not find it too bad once you start.'

Churchill exploded with rage. With his fist crashing on the table, words tumbled out in a furious torrent, much too fast for the interpreter to relay. Stalin threw back his head and roared with laughter.

LEFT: Churchill celebrates the Allied landings on Sicily in June 1943 outside 10 Downing Street.

RIGHT: With President Truman (centre) and Stalin at the Potsdam conference in 1945 – Churchill was forced to leave after eight days because of his party's defeat in the general election.

'I do not know what you are saying,' he interrupted. 'But I like your attitude!'

The incident signalled a new warmth in Anglo-Soviet relations which was not lost until the Cold War. But Churchill's – and Britain's – significance in the world arena was inevitably diminished after the arrival of Roosevelt and Stalin. He described himself as 'the poor little English donkey' between the Russian bear and the American buffalo during the summit meetings. But he was convinced that he was 'the only one who knew the right way home'.

Churchill remained beguiled by the Anglo-American 'special relationship'. He even envisaged a common citizenship between the two countries after the end of the war. And, despite their common purpose, he never rubbed along with Free French leader General de Gaulle. 'We all have our cross to bear,' he said. 'Mine is the cross of Lorraine'. (The cross of Lorraine was the symbol adopted by the Free French.)

It seems like the plot of an overimaginative thriller, but in 1943 the Nazis attempted to poison Churchill. Secret agents known as Max-men were planning an assassination as the prime minister returned from a visit to Turkey through the Mediterranean and North Africa. A radio message from the German secret service was intercepted, allowing Churchill's deputy, Clement Attlee, to wire him with a blunt message: 'Attempts are going to be made to bump you off'. It was 'essential' Churchill cut short the tour, which he duly did.

Throughout 1943, Allied planes rained bombs on Germany, causing wholesale loss of life. Churchill's daughter Sarah was working in RAF intelligence and realised the scale of destruction. Shaken to the core, she told her father about the shocking loss of life. And far from dismissing her anxieties, Churchill shared them. Not for the first time, he questioned the use of aerial warfare.

Watching film footage of a British raid on a German city, he once asked: 'Are we beasts? Are we taking this too far?' His conclusion, however, was always the same. It wasGermany who had begun the destruction

LEFT: The Potsdam conference completed the carve-up of Central and Eastern Europe in Soviet and American spheres of influence begun by Roosevelt, Churchill and Stalin at Yalta earlier in the same year. By the end of the conference, only Stalin remained of those who had met at Yalta.

RIGHT: The prime minister leaves Downing Street for the V-E Day celebrations.

of Europe's fine cities – Warsaw in 1939 and Rotterdam in 1940 were devestated by German bombers. Now the beleaguered country was reaping its grim reward.

Much of the first half of 1944 was spent in preparation for D-day, the invasion of France by the Allies. Churchill was at last convinced that the time was ripe for another front in Europe.

The success of D-day is well documented. That was thanks to a happy coincidence of many factors. The plans were kept strictly secret, which was astonishing when full-scale rehearsals were being staged around the British coast. While the Germans knew an invasion was coming, they didn't know where or precisely when – and a bogus invasion force helped to maintain the secret. German intelligence was fooled by the mighty deception which had tent cities and entire ports constructed to mask the true intentions of the Allies.

There was one other piece of brilliant planning: the invention and construction of Mulberry harbours, which helped to land the invasion force, and PLUTO (pipeline under the ocean), which kept them supplied with fuel. The genius behind both of them was Churchill.

Operation Overlord was the key single action of the war by the North Atlantic allies; although many of the strategic moves which took place in the lead-up to it were partly responsible for its success, including air raids on railway yards in northern France and on Germany's oil industry. The cost of Overlord was high. Between 6 June and 25 August 1944, out of some 2,000,000 Allied soldiers were landed in Normandy, 215,000 became casualties.

Churchill – perhaps because of his unfortunate Gallipoli experience in 1915 – had carefully followed every aspect of the D-day plans and became an expert on everything from the waterproofing of tanks to the techniques of naval bombardment. Supremely confident of its outcome, he wrote in his diary afterwards: 'We had the mastery of the oceans and of the air. The Hitler tyranny was doomed.'

Churchill even planned to make the crossing with the troops but General Dwight D. Eisenhower, the Allied commander, refused to countenance it. Churchill was determined, telling him: 'By shipping myself as a bona-fide member of a ship's company it would be beyond your authority to prevent my going.' It was a letter from King George VI himself which finally put paid to the idea. Was it right for the prime minister to take part in the invasion when the king himself had a greater claim to a place aboard ship?

Disappointed, Churchill stood down. Yet just six days later he crossed the Channel, viewed the new battlefields and talked to the British and Empire troops who had overrun objectives such as Caen.

With the success of Operation Overlord pressing Germany from the west and the Red Army steamroller bearing down from the east, it was only a matter of time before Germany capitulated. After the Germans' last, desperate throw, the Ardennes offensive, the invading armies crossed the Rhine. Churchill was there in March 1945 to cross the river by landing craft, watch the continuing advance and discuss tactics with Supreme Commander Eisenhower.

Churchill tried to persuade Eisenhower to race for Berlin in order to prevent the Russians assuming control of Eastern Europe. Somewhat treacherously but entirely accurately, he wished to deny his Soviet allies the right to present themselves as 'an overwhelming contributor to our common victory'.

Eisenhower was unable to accede to these entreaties, since President Roosevelt had now become utterly suspicious of Britain's 'imperialist' ambitions. Blind to the looming tyranny of Communism – and debilitated by cancer – the US President trusted Joseph Stalin more than he did his old ally Winston

Left: Churchill and the king and queen acknowledge the cheers of the crowd on V-E day.

Right: The relief that the war in Europe is at an end is palpable in this *Daily Mail* headline.

Daily Mail
4 A.M. EDITION
NO. 15,290 ONE PENNY
FOR KING AND EMPIRE
TUESDAY, MAY 8, 1945

3-POWER ANNOUNCEMENT TO-DAY; BUT BRITAIN KNEW LAST NIGHT

VE-DAY—IT'S ALL OVER

All quiet till 9 p.m.—then the London crowds went mad in the West End

By Day ↑

↓ By Night

THE Face of Victory — by day and night: Roadways around Piccadilly Circus were jammed nearly solid yesterday afternoon by crowds waiting to hear VE-Day announced. Then they decided not to wait — they began to celebrate. These Daily Mail pictures give you a vivid impression of the great concourse of joy — above by day; on the left, by night. Other scenes — Pages THREE and FOUR.

PM put off the big speech

UNTIL TO-DAY

By Wilson Broadbent, Diplomatic Correspondent

GERMANY surrendered unconditionally to the Allies yesterday. But there will be no official announcement of victory until 3 p.m. today — officially described as VE-Day — when Mr Churchill will give the news to the world.

He will follow this with an address to the House of Commons, and at 9 p.m. the King will speak to Britain and the Empire. Mr Churchill's private room at the House of Commons was last night 'wired up' so that if he wishes he can make his broadcast from there.

To-day's announcement will be made simultaneously in London, Washington and Moscow. To-day, therefore, is the first of the promised two-days VE-holiday for the country.

Broadcasts will also be made by General Eisenhower and Field Marshals Montgomery and Alexander.

Mr Churchill's two statements to-day will not affect his intention to broadcast at length on Thursday night, the fifth anniversary of his assumption of the Premiership.

Everything ready

After his statement in the House of Commons, Mr Churchill will propose the adjournment of business while MPs attend a special Service of Thanksgiving at St Margaret's Church, Westminster. They will then return to the House of Commons, adjourn, and arrange to meet again on Wednesday.

Until just before 6 o'clock last night it was fully expected that Mr Churchill would be able to announce the news that the war was over.

He had been standing by the microphone from some time after 3 o'clock, and everything was ready for him to break into the normal programmes of the BBC.

Earlier in the day he had been speaking on the

BACK PAGE—Col FIVE

U.S. made it VE-Day all the same

Work walk-out

From Don Iddon, Daily Mail Correspondent

NEW YORK, Monday

THIS was VE-Day in the U.S. — official or not.

The celebrations began in New York at breakfast-time, a few minutes after word came from Rheims, France, that Germany had surrendered unconditionally to Britain, the United States, and Russia.

They went on all day despite an avalanche of confused messages, lack of official confirmation, half-denials, and a barrage of rumours that the surrender was a hoax.

First reaction

The American public, and particularly the New York public, this time was determined that this was the end of the war in Europe, and resolved to commemorate it.

The first reaction, and it

BACK PAGE—Col THREE

Daily Mail

IN accordance with the expressed desire of the Government that workers generally should enjoy a day's holiday following the announcement of the cessa-

SYMBOL of the mood of London: This man has climbed to the top of a lamp-post and is waving a flag above the crowds.—Daily Mail picture.

GOEBBELS' BODY IN A SHELTER

GOEBBELS, the German Propaganda Minister, his wife, and five children have been found dead in Berlin.

Moscow says that their bodies were found in an air-raid shelter near the Reichstag, and it has been established that all died of poisoning.

No trace has been found of the bodies of Hitler or Göring. out, however, that their bodies may have been destroyed in the wreckage of the burning Chancellery or some other building.

Moscow radio last night reported, says B.U.P., that troops had penetrated deep into an underground fortress in the basement of Hitler's Chancellery.

Beacon chain begun by Piccadilly's bonfires

By Guy Ramsey

LONDON, dead from six until nine, suddenly broke into victory life last night. Suddenly, spontaneously, deliriously. The people of London, denied VE-Day officially, held their own jubilation. "VE-Day may be to-morrow," they said, "but the war is over to-night." Bonfires blazed from Piccadilly to Wapping.

The sky once lit by the glare of the blitz shone red with the Victory glow. The last trains departed from the West End unregarded. The pent-up spirits of the throng, the polyglot throng that is London in war-time, burst out, and by 11 o'clock the capital was ablaze with enthusiasm.

Processions formed up out of nowhere, disintegrating for no reason, to re-form somewhere else. Waving flags, marching in step, with linked arms or half-embraced, the people strode down the great thoroughfares — Piccadilly, Regent Street, the Mall, to the portals of Buckingham Palace.

They marched and counter-marched so as not to get too far from the centre. And from them, in harmony and discord, rose song. The songs of the last war, the songs of a century ago. The songs of the beginning of this war — "Roll out the Barrel" and "Tipperary"; "Ilkla Moor" and "Loch Lomond"; "Bless 'em All" and "Pack Up Your Troubles."

ROCKETS AND SONGS

Rockets — found no-one knows where, set-off by no-one knows whom — streaked into the sky, exploding not in death but a burst of scarlet fire. A pile of straw filled with thunder-flashes salvaged from some military dump spurted and exploded near Leicester Square.

Every car that challenged the milling, moiling throng was submerged in humanity. They climbed on the running-boards, on the bonnet, on the roof. They hammered on the panels. They shouted and sang.

Against the drumming on metal came the clash of cymbals, improvised out of dustbin lids. The dustbin itself was a football for an impromptu Rugger scrum. Bubbling, exploding with gaiety, the people "mafficked." Headlights silhouetted couples kissing, couples cheering, couples waving flags.

MONTY MEETS ROKOSSOVSKY

4 toasts at lunch

TWENTY-FIRST ARMY GROUP, Monday. — Field Marshal Montgomery lunched to-day with Marshal Konstantin Rokossovsky at Wismar.

Toasts were drunk to the Allied armies, Mr Churchill, Marshal Stalin, and President Truman. — *Reuter.*

ARRESTED POLES MAY BE TRIED BY LUBLIN

LUBLIN radio said yesterday that the Polish Provisional Government may demand that General Okulicki and others of the 16 Poles arrested by the Russians be tried both in Warsaw and Moscow for high treason.

The radio said: 'Public opinion in Poland has received with indignation the news of the action of Okulicki and his accomplices who are accused of carrying out diversionary activities directed against the re-born Polish State, it constitutes high treason.

'The Provisional Government reserves the right to demand that Okulicki and his accomplices be turned over to the Polish authorities to be indicted in the courts of the Republic as well.'

Mr Mikolajczyk, former Polish Prime Minister in London, announced yesterday that he is preparing a statement on the arrests.

He said that the arrested

Churchill. When Roosevelt died in April and the more anti-Communist Harry S. Truman took over the presidency, it was too late. Hitler shot himself in his Berlin bunker as the Red Army swept into Berlin – and across half of Europe

When Hitler's forces were finally vanquished in the west and Britain's Field Marshal Bernard Montgomery had accepted the German surrender, Churchill broadcast to the world on V-E Day, 8 May 1945: 'Hostilities will end officially at one minute after midnight tonight, but in the interests of saving lives the "Cease Fire" began yesterday, to be sounded all along the front… Advance Britannia. Long live the cause of freedom. God Save the King.'

Then an elated Winston stood on a balcony overlooking Whitehall. The cheers seemed endless. They reverberated throughout every city in the land. Nowhere were they louder than when the king, Queen Mary and their princesses Elizabeth and Margaret waved at the throng from the balcony of Buckingham Palace. Ushered out to take his bow at the centre of the Royal Family was the rotund and beaming figure of His Majesty's prime minister.

Churchill was vindicated, and his goodwill extended to all – except Nazis. He wrote:

> Today, perhaps, we shall think mostly of ourselves. Tomorrow we shall pay a particular tribute to our Russian comrades whose prowess in the field has been one of the grand contributions to the general victory. After gallant France had been struck down we, from this island and from our united Empire, maintained the struggle single-handed for a whole year until we were joined by the military might of Soviet Russia and later by the overwhelming power and resources of the United States of America. Finally almost the whole world was combined against the evil-doers who are now prostrate before us.

Churchill remained concerned for the fate of the British and Empire troops fighting on against Japan and looked forward to victory there, too. The triumph came – but only after Churchill had been removed from office by the electorate he had saved from the German jackboot.

Left: One wild party – delighted Britons celebrate V-E day in Piccadilly Circus.

A DAY'S WORK

In 1942 Winston suffered a mild stroke, kept secret for years. Afterwards, he looked slightly more jaded although he was still filled with the same energy. When he was not out visiting the troops or air bases or bombed civilians, his daily regime was strict, though eccentric.

He would awake at 8 a.m., light his first cigar of the day and take his first whisky of the day, heavily diluted with soda water. Breakfast, taken in bed, would be ample: kedgeree or, whenever possible, grouse. While eating, resplendent in green-and-gold silk dressing gown, he would read the morning papers (for the second time, having read the early editions the night before).

Churchill usually remained in bed, surrounded by secretaries, as he answered telegrams, ploughed through his black dispatch box and issued his orders for the day. Rising at noon, he would normally have a working lunch with politicians, diplomats or military top brass – the exception being Tuesdays when he always dined privately with King George VI. When the Buckingham Palace air raid sirens sounded, the pair would be seen strolling to the shelter, glasses and plates of food still in their hands.

BELOW: Cecil Beaton, official photographer to the rich and famous, took this portrait of the prime minister in 1941.

Left: Churchill speaks at Burnley football ground during the 1945 election. He was unprepared for Labour's demand to hold a ballot immediately after Germany had surrendered.

Right: This portrait was painted in 1943 by Egerton Cooper, and hung in the Carlton Club, the exclusive Conservative social society.

The afternoon's business was done in his George Street offices near Downing Street. Beneath them were the bunkers where his War Cabinet met daily. Late every afternoon, Churchill catnapped for an hour, 'by which means I am able to press a day-and-a-half's work into one'.

Parliamentary debates would follow in the evening, with dinner taken in the basement of 10 Downing Street with military and parliamentary colleagues. As they retired for the night, Winston would continue working until at least two and often four o'clock in the morning.

His last act before bed was usually to send a wire to President Roosevelt with his latest report, request or good idea. Because of the time difference, the reply would normally be awaiting him when he awoke. Roosevelt once said: 'You know, Winston has a hundred ideas every day, and one of them is almost sure to be right.'

THE FINAL YEARS

WINSTON Churchill resigned as prime minister on 23 May 1945 in order that the first general election in 10 years might take place. His coalition government was dissolved. He had hoped to maintain the status quo until the Japanese were defeated but Labour was ready to throw off the old order and meet new challenges.

Despite his age – he was now 71 – Churchill had not lost his taste for politics. But he had clearly lost some of the flair. As he campaigned for the Tories that summer, he claimed that a Labour government would have some form of Gestapo to enforce its policies. Grateful though the population might have been to Churchill for his inspired leadership during conflict, most found the analogy an odious one. Labour was promising a welfare state, already introduced in part, while the Tories prevaricated on the issue. There was disquiet too at the division of peacetime Europe, which Churchill had helped draw up. The USSR won control of large chunks of the Continent, including half of Germany.

When the results of the election were announced on 26 July 1945, Labour had won a landslide victory. Clement Attlee was now prime minister.

Clementine tried to soothe her husband with the words: 'It may well be a blessing in disguise.'

'At the moment it seems quite effectively disguised,' he retorted.

And to those who tried to comfort him with talk of a high-ranking reward for his wartime service, perhaps the Order of the Garter, Winston responded: 'Why should I accept the Order of the Garter from his Majesty when the people have just given me the order of the boot?'

LEFT: Churchill's prominence as war leader was dwarfed by the votes of millions as the Conservatives were defeated in the 1945 election.

RIGHT: The great man is cheered by a crowd of Tories during the campaign in which he warned of a Labour 'Gestapo' enforcing socialist policies.

FLOWERS
WORKS
PRINTING
WORKS
Flowers
BOOKSELLERS AND STATIONERS
DAYS

Left: A tired Clementine sits on the platform as Churchill speaks during the 1945 election.

Churchill was also suffering a major blow in his personal life. Chartwell, the home he loved dearly, had fallen into decay through the war years. Post-war rationing meant there was a shortage of materials to restore it. So in 1946, a group of Churchill's friends bought Chartwell and handed it over to the National Trust, on condition that the Churchills be allowed to remain in residence until their death. This ensured the estate would become a memorial to the great war leader. Churchill later expanded the Chartwell estate by buying a further 500 acres to begin farming.

Churchill was still feted everywhere he went around the world. In September 1946, he enjoyed a triumphant reception in Zurich. But he found such accolades insufficient solace for his loss of political power at home.

He made one more famous speech, in 1946. It echoed his belief that Europe was a 'rubble heap' incapable of defending itself against the encroachment of Soviet power. Churchill had set himself a twin goal: to counteract American isolationism, persuading Washington to throw its weight into the balance against the Soviet Union, and to promote Western European unity as a defence against the spread of Communism. In his speech in Fulton, Missouri, in the presence of President Harry Truman, Churchill memorably pronounced: 'From Stettin on the Baltic to Trieste on the Adriatic, an iron curtain has descended over the continent... There is nothing they [the Russians] admire so much as strength and nothing for which they have less respect than military weakness.'

It was an unpopular speech at a time when the Soviet Union was still regarded as an ally of the West. But two years later, as tension between the United States and the Soviet Union dramatically increased, Churchill was praised for his prophetic insight. The speech is often interpreted as the first salvo in the Cold War, and gave the world the term 'Iron Curtain'.

RIGHT: Churchill addresses a crowd of Tory supporters at Walthamstow Stadium during the 1945 election.

RIGHT: In 1946, Churchill attended the play *Fifty Fifty* with the duchess of Marlborough (left).

Churchill was determined that life away from the main political platform should not be empty. His major project was to write his own version of the origins and conduct of the Second World War. The first part of this six-volume historical epic appeared in 1948. These war memories were eventually to earn him a Nobel Prize for literature. But they also made him a rich man. He bought two adjoining houses in Hyde Park Gate and kept a suite of rooms at the Savoy Hotel to be near parliament.

In 1949, Churchill bought a string of racehorses and enjoyed considerable successes, his Colonist II winning at Ascot. He was also, by now, spending more time abroad, especially in warmer climes such as the south of France or Morocco. The cold damp of British winters was bad for his failing health. He had already suffered the first of a series of strokes.

If after the war the country had turned against Churchill as the leader of a political party, England and the world still acknowledged with eternal thanks his pre-eminence as wartime leader, statesman and celebrity. Honours were still showered on him, including the Grotius medal for services in the cause of peace and an honorary degree from Cambridge University.

Throughout these years in opposition, some Tories questioned the wisdom of keeping such an aged leader at their helm. Was not Anthony Eden a better candidate to carry the party back into power? Churchill was unmoved. 'When I want to tease Anthony, I remind him that Gladstone formed his last administration at the age of 88', Churchill said mischievously.

In any case, the Labour tide was ebbing. Their majority at the 1950 election was down to five seats. On 26 October 1951, Churchill was back at 10 Downing Street, forming his first peacetime government – at the age of 77 – with a majority of 16 seats.

Despite his advancing years, Churchill's second term as prime minister was a determined and demanding one. He backed the agreement that ended the Korean War and helped persuade America not to intervene to

Left: Churchill was given plenty of honours after his party's electoral defeat in 1945. Here he thanks the people of Manchester for giving him the freedom of the city in 1947.

ABOVE: The French prime minister, Paul Ramadier, embraces Churchill after presenting him with the Medaille Militaire in 1947.

RIGHT: Churchill took a cruise with Clementine on the *Queen Elizabeth* in 1947.

rescue the French from Ho Chi Minh's guerrilla army. He had to help in the rearmament of Germany and support the independent Chinese state of Formosa (now Taiwan). He saw the emergence of Mau Mau terrorism in Kenya and watched the insidious spread of Communism throughout the former colonial countries of the world. Frustratingly, his major objective, to organise a summit meeting at which America, the Soviet Union and Britain would resolve outstanding differences, was not to be.

On 24 April 1953, the Queen conferred upon the Right Honourable Winston Churchill, MP the honour of knighthood. Later that year, he was also installed as a member of the Order of the Garter.

Churchill's 80th birthday in November 1954 brought tributes and gifts from all over the world. A birthday fund, originated by a group of private citizens, received contributions on a scale never known before. Gifts of flowers, money, wine, cigars and personal souvenirs connected with incidents in his past, flooded in to 10 Downing Street.

Official celebrations took the form of two presentations in Westminster Hall. One presentation was that of an illuminated address, signed by almost every MP who had served under Churchill. The other, on behalf

LEFT: In 1949, he celebrated the sale of one of his paintings to a Brazilian newspaper owner who paid £1310 10s for *The Blue Sitting Room, Trent Park*.

RIGHT: Bernard Baruch (left), the powerfully connected US financier and economic adviser, is welcomed by Churchill on the occasion of his visit to London in 1949.

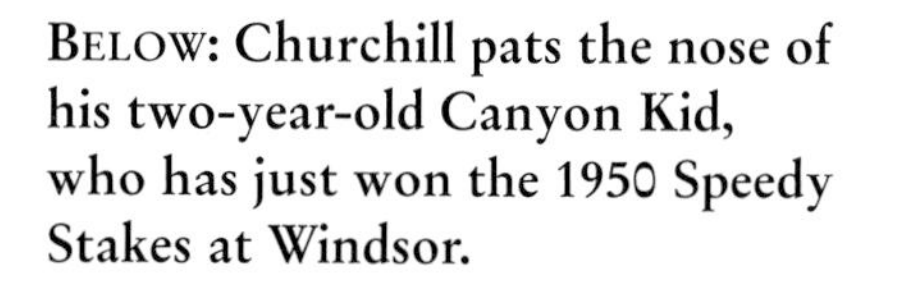

BELOW: Churchill pats the nose of his two-year-old Canyon Kid, who has just won the 1950 Speedy Stakes at Windsor.

LEFT: Jockey Terry Hawcroft talks to Churchill after riding the former prime minister's horse Colonist II to victory in the 1949 Lime Tree Stakes at Windsor.

OPPOSITE TOP LEFT: Montgomery and Churchill sit together during the El Alamein anniversary celebrated at Earl's Court in 1949.

OPPOSITE TOP RIGHT: Churchill arrives in Manchester to give a speech during the 1950 election, the second fought by the Conservatives under his leadership.

OPPOSITE BELOW LEFT: A wistful-looking Churchill – perhaps pondering his sunset years? – sits in the grounds of Chartwell with his eventual successor as Conservative leader, Sir Anthony Eden.

OPPOSITE BELOW RIGHT: In April 1951 Churchill paid a visit to Sheffield. In six months he would be back at 10 Downing Street as prime minister.

of the Lords and the Commons, was a portrait painted by Graham Sutherland. This was a controversial gift, for both Churchill and Clementine hated modern art. They also felt the portrait made Churchill look too old and ravaged. The picture was hidden away at Chartwell until Clementine destroyed it in 1956.

Churchill welcomed the Queen to Downing Street for the last time as her prime minister on 4 April 1955. The next day he stood down from office and was succeeded by his supporter from the days of Munich, Anthony Eden. On 6 April, cheered by his staff, Churchill left Downing Street for Chartwell. His comment to the press was: 'It's always nice to come home.'

Clementine told friends a different story. She said: 'Retirement is his first death – for him a death in life.'

Churchill was not invited by his party to play any significant role in the election campaign of May 1955. Although he officially remained as MP for Woodford until 1964 and occasionally occupied his seat in the Commons, he never again addressed the House on a political issue. Churchill's last significant political act came after Eden's resignation in 1957, when he advised the Queen to invite Harold Macmillan, rather than Richard 'Rab' Butler, to form the next government.

With his role as statesman now reduced to only ceremonial appearances, Churchill returned to his second greatest passion, writing. He completed *A History of the English-Speaking Peoples*, in four volumes. He still painted and played cards, dividing his time between his beloved Chartwell and the French Riviera. But deep down, Churchill was severely depressed through these declining years. He became withdrawn and sullen.

Nevertheless, he continued to receive honours for a life in politics. In 1956 he was awarded the Charlemagne prize for his services to Europe. He went to Paris to receive the Croix de la Liberation from General de Gaulle in 1958, and visited President Eisenhower in the United States. But a series of minor

strokes progressively weakened his mental agility. In 1960 he suffered a serious fall in Monte Carlo, breaking a bone in his neck. In 1962 he broke his thigh. Surrounded by a coterie of nursing staff and private aides, Churchill became morose and immobile.

His daughter Diana committed suicide in 1964, but by then Churchill was too senile to take in the tragedy. After a final stroke, Churchill died at his London home near Hyde Park on the morning of Sunday 24 January 1965, coincidentally the 70th anniversary of the death of his father. Winston Churchill had survived to the ripe old age of 90.

The Queen had always said she would honour Churchill with a state funeral – the first since the duke of Wellington's in 1852. Over 300,000 people queued in bitterly cold weather to file past Churchill's body lying in state for three days in Westminster. Millions witnessed the funeral, either in person or on television on 30 January, as the procession made its way from Westminster to St Paul's Cathedral.

Churchill, in his long, controversial but incredible life, had become a public monument. Even his political enemies felt affection for this great statesman.

Churchill was buried alongside his parents in Bladon churchyard, within sight of his birthplace, Blenheim Palace. Two wreaths were left on the grave. One, from Clementine, was inscribed: 'To my Darling Winston. Clemmie.' The other, from the Queen, read: 'From the Nation and Commonwealth. In grateful remembrance. Elizabeth R.'

LEFT: Churchill celebrated his 77th birthday in 10 Downing Street on 30 November 1951, just over a month after his party achieved a Commons majority.

OPPOSITE TOP LEFT: General Eisenhower, then military commander of NATO, helps Churchill get around during the 1951 El Alamein reunion.

OPPOSITE TOP RIGHT: Churchill, dressed in the full regalia of the chancellor of Bristol University, attends a ceremony awarding honorary degrees.

OPPOSITE: Churchill and Clementine return to Downing Street after an official engagement.

Above: Churchill sits with Ambassador Sir Ronald Lindsay on a visit to the British embassy in Washington, DC, in 1952.

Left: Churchill is led to the christening of one grandson, Jeremy Soames, by another, Christopher Soames Jr, whose father was the last governor of the colony of Rhodesia (1979-80).

RIGHT: On Coronation Day in 1953, the prime minister attended the ceremony with his grandson Winston, who himself was later a Conservative MP.

BELOW: Sir Winston arrives at St George's Chapel at Windsor Castle for the Garter Service.

LEFT: Churchill thanks the audience at Westminster Hall after being presented with a portrait by Graham Sutherland on the occasion of his 80th birthday. Both he and Clemmie disliked the painting, and Clemmie later burned it.

RIGHT: Churchill addresses the Conservative party conference as prime minister for the last time in October 1954. On 5 April 1955 he resigned.

BELOW: Churchill leaves 10 Downing Street for Westminster Hall to celebrate his 80th birthday.

Above Left: Churchill hands power over to Sir Anthony Eden in April 1955.

Above: Churchill sets sail for a cruise on Aristotle Onassis's yacht. Tina Onassis waves goodbye to the photographers.

Left: The two-fingered salute pursues him around the world, even in Italy.

RIGHT: Little love was lost during wartime between Churchill and Free French leader Charles De Gaulle. But in 1958, the Frenchman gave the former prime minister the Croix de la Libération.

BELOW: In retirement, Churchill could still welcome distinguished callers such as Prime Minister Harold Macmillan (left) and Bernard Baruch (right).

Left: Churchill leaves his Hyde Park Gate home for the south of France in the spring of 1962. As his health deteriorated in old age, Churchill spent more time in warmer climates.

Below Left: A broken thigh in 1962 left Churchill morose and irritable, and requiring almost constant nursing attention.

Below: Lady Churchill helped her husband cope with a trying old age as he lost his vitality and retired from his public offices.

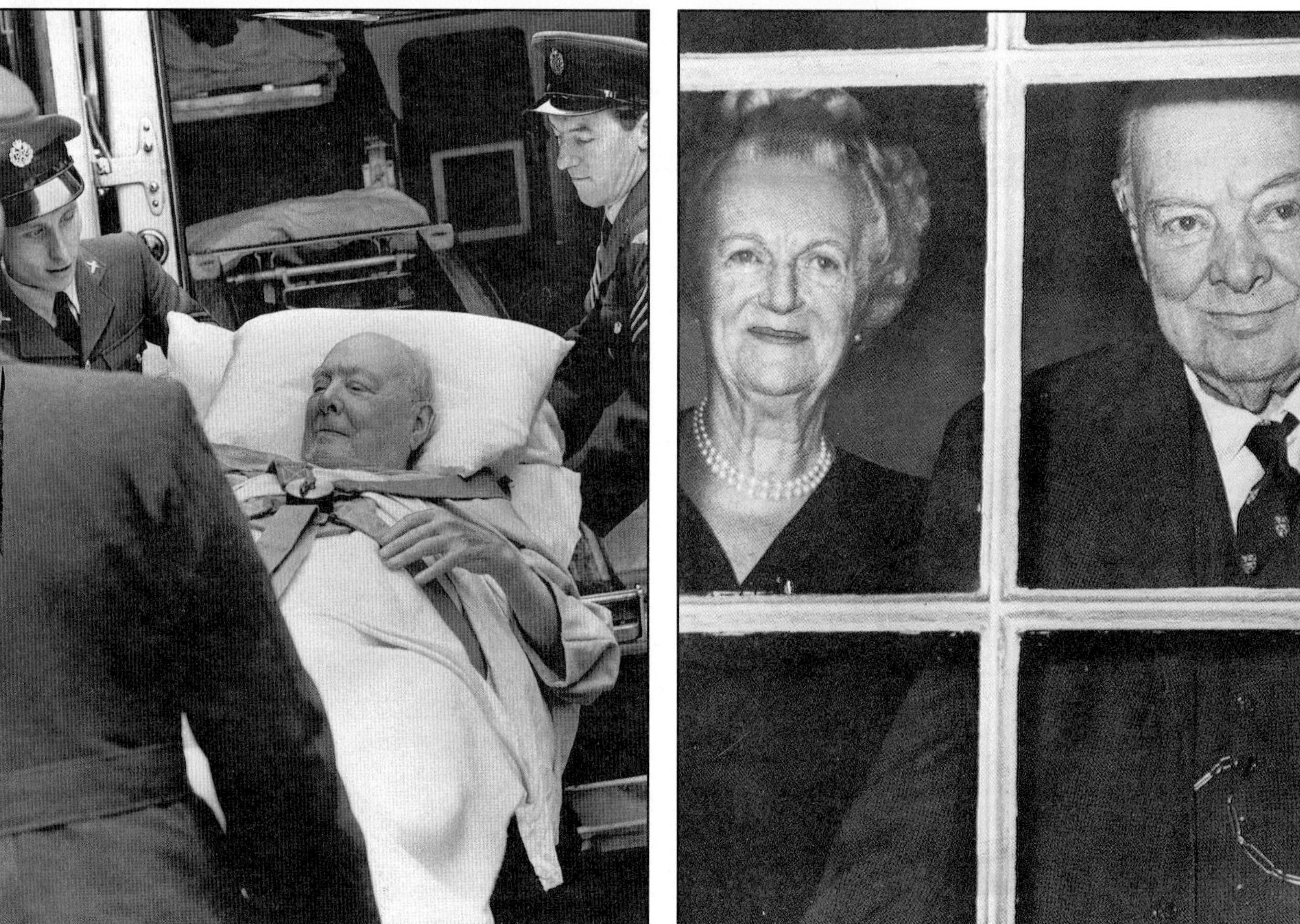

ABOVE: Although Churchill received a state funeral in St Paul's Cathedral, he was buried in a small churchyard near Blenheim Palace.

RIGHT: Churchill and Clementine are buried beside Winston's parents in Blaydon churchyard.

Principal Dates

1874	Born at Blenheim Palace (30 November)
1888	Enters Harrow School
1893	Enters Sandhurst
1895	Joins 4th Hussars; war correspondent in Cuba
1897	Joins Malakand Field Force
1898	Joins Nile Expeditionary Force
1899	Held prisoner in Pretoria but escapes
1900	Becomes Conservative MP for Oldham
1904	Joins Liberals
1908	President of the Board of Trade; marries Clementine Ogilvy Hozier
1910	Home Secretary
1911	Siege of Sidney Street; becomes first lord of the Admiralty
1915	Disastrous Gallipoli campaign
1917	Becomes Lloyd George's minister for munitions
1918	Secretary of state for war and air
1924	Returns to Conservative fold; becomes chancellor of Exchequer
1931	Conservatives return to power leading National government; Churchill not invited to join
1936	Backs Edward VIII in Abdication crisis
1938	Attacks Chamberlain's Munich appeasement of Hitler
1939	War declared (3 September); Churchill returns as first lord of the Admiralty
1940	Chamberlain loses vote of confidence; Churchill prime minister of Coalition government; surrender of France; Dunkirk; Battle of Britain; start of the Blitz
1941	Rommel sweeps through Africa; Atlantic Charter with Roosevelt; Pearl Harbor
1942	El Alamein
1943	German cities bombed
1944	Invasion of Normandy
1945	Victory in Europe (8 May); Churchill cheered through London; loses general election in Labour landslide
1951	Churchill back as prime minister, aged 77
1953	Awarded knighthood and order of the Garter
1955	Retires as prime minister, succeeded by Anthony Eden
1964	Retires as MP
1965	Dies (24 January) aged 90